FEARLESS LEADERSHIP

HIGH-PERFORMANCE LESSONS
FROM THE FLIGHT DECK

CAREY D. LOHRENZ

GREENLEAF
BOOK GROUP PRESS

Published by Greenleaf Book Group Press
Austin, Texas
www.gbgpress.com

Copyright ©2014 Carey Lohrenz Enterprises, LLC.

All rights reserved.

No part of this book may be reproduced, stored in a retrieval system, or
transmitted by any means, electronic, mechanical, photocopying, recording,
or otherwise, without written permission from the copyright holder.

Distributed by Greenleaf Book Group

For ordering information or special discounts for bulk purchases, please contact
Greenleaf Book Group at PO Box 91869, Austin, TX 78709, 512.891.6100.

Design and composition by Greenleaf Book Group
Cover design by Greenleaf Book Group
Author photo by Allison Rodgers
U.S. Navy Photo by Carly Joy Cranston

Cataloging-in-Publication data
Lohrenz, Carey D.
  Fearless leadership: high-performance lessons from the flight deck / Carey D.
Lohrenz.—First edition.
    pages ; cm
  Issued also as an ebook.
  Includes bibliographical references.
  1. Lohrenz, Carey D. 2. Leadership. 3. Courage. 4. Management. 5. Teams in
the workplace. I. Title.
HD57.7 .L674 2014
658.4/092   2014933691

ISBN 13: 978-1-62634-113-5

Part of the Tree Neutral® program, which offsets the number of trees
consumed in the production and printing of this book by taking
proactive steps, such as planting trees in direct proportion to the
number of trees used: www.treeneutral.com

TreeNeutral

Printed in the United States of America on acid-free paper

16 17 18 19 20   10 9 8 7 6 5 4

First Edition

Dedication

Our country allows for great privileges. I am deeply grateful that mine was being able to serve. An anonymous person once wrote, "A veteran is someone who, at one point in his or her life, wrote a blank check made payable to 'The United States of America,' for an amount of 'up to and including my life.'" To all veterans, thank you.

To my kids, Alexandra, Annabelle, Dalton, and Danielle: Wherever life takes you, be fearless.

CONTENTS

WHAT IS FEARLESS LEADERSHIP?

There can be no great accomplishment without risk.
—Neil Armstrong

July 11, 1994, approximately 250 nautical miles southwest of Japan. While approaching the USS *Kitty Hawk* in severe pitching-deck conditions, an F-14 Tomcat strikes the flight deck ramp, breaking in two and exploding into a fireball. Part of the aircraft slides off the flight deck, while most of the fuselage remains on deck—engulfed in flames. Both crewmembers successfully eject, but to the horror of hundreds of onlookers, the pilot lands directly in the inferno. His life is saved thanks to the quick and fearless reactions of the firefighting crew. A former classmate and friend of mine, he is severely burned and will spend months in a critical care burn unit, fighting for his life. That fiery disaster is forever engraved in my memory.

A few days later and thousands of miles away, it's a pitch-black summer night and I'm rocketing through the darkness over a nondescript patch of the Pacific Ocean in the same type of plane: a 72,000-pound Grumman F-14 Tomcat strike fighter. In 1994, it's the premier supersonic strike fighter, the most lethal in the world—glamorous but dangerous. The F-14 is the primary defender of the naval battle group on the ocean below (made up of an aircraft carrier—the USS *Abraham Lincoln*—and its escorts), and it can carry six AIM-54 Phoenix missiles, each with a range of more than one hundred miles, to provide superior long-range intercept capabilities.

The Tomcat carries a wide range of other ordnance, too, including Sidewinder, Sparrow, and AMRAAM missiles and a 20mm M61A Vulcan Gatling machine gun capable of unleashing six thousand rounds per minute. The craft is also modified and upgraded to deliver a variety of bombs, earning it the affectionate nickname "Bombcat." And as the recon eyes of the fleet, we Tomcat pilots utilize the Tactical Airborne Reconnaissance Pod System (TARPS), a camera pod mounted to the underside of the Tomcat that scans the terrain slipping by below. This is a flexible, highly capable aircraft, the envy of most armed forces in the world.

All those fantastic capabilities and all that firepower aside, outside my strike fighter as I fly tonight, all I see is inky black—the word *dark* doesn't even begin to describe it. You could try to replicate this darkness by turning off all the lights in your house at midnight, then walking into a closet in a windowless room, closing the door, and blindfolding yourself. And then blindfolding yourself again. Somehow, it still wouldn't be quite as dark.

As my fighter jet tears through the night, I think about the task waiting for me below: I have to land this thing, and it's not going to be easy. It never is. Just ahead, invisible to me, the aircraft carrier is bobbing on a choppy ocean. An aircraft carrier might seem like a big thing, but not from my perspective, not right now. To me, cruising through the impenetrable blackness at roughly 350 miles per hour, the carrier seems about the size of a discarded postage stamp—and I have to land on it. I won't have the luxury of six to ten thousand feet of runway, as a military or commercial flight landing at an airport would have. I'll have roughly *three hundred* feet. This is not a task for the faint of heart.

In fact, landing a fighter jet on an aircraft carrier at night is the most harrowing maneuver in all of military aviation. The tension, anxiety, and fear that every carrier aviator feels as he or she works to get safely aboard are intense, genuine and need to be controlled. Throw in the fact that, in the case of an emergency, there's often no other place to land, and you have a recipe for a real nail-biter. We call these "blue-water operations"—flights we attempt when the carrier is far out to sea and the jet can't carry enough fuel to get us to a land-based runway—and they're the ultimate test.

You can actually taste your own fear as you descend toward the pitching deck knowing the back end of the ship is bobbing up and down in thirty-foot rises and falls. The conditions seem horrific even to the aviators who are safely below the carrier deck, watching all this unfold on the ship's closed-circuit TV. You'd be hard-pressed to find one aviator whose palms aren't sweaty just from watching. Weak knees, rapid heart rates, slight waves of nausea—they're all present as the bystanders summon up their courage. After all, they'll be the next ones lifting off into the night.

The really fun part of this flight happened about an hour and a half ago, during the catapult launch, more commonly known as a takeoff. For a fighter pilot like me, waiting my turn to get hurled off the front end of an aircraft carrier is like being a five-year-old at Christmas—times twenty-five. It is that fun and the anticipation is killer. A catapult launch in an F-14 Tomcat is sheer exhilaration. At that point, the excitement hasn't yet turned to fear.

Waiting in my aircraft behind a jet blast deflector (a metal fence that rises up behind the jet engine to deflect its exhaust) as another F-14 Tomcat pushes up the throttles to maximum power and gets launched off the flight deck—it's nothing short of amazing. As the afterburner kicks in and the fighter jet in front of me kicks out 35,000 pounds of thrust, I can feel the pressure and reverberation through my whole body. It's not just a little buzzing; it's like being in the front row at an AC/DC concert, smack-dab in front of the biggest speaker, the bass amplified times ten as it pounds through me. The exhaust from that jet's engines fills my cockpit. All of my instruments go wild. The warning and caution lights, overwhelmed by the heat blasting over the fuselage, flash frantically.

Then the jet blast deflector drops back down, and I'm up next. This isn't *Top Gun*, *Iron Eagle*, or *Stealth*—this is real life. I'm preparing for the unmatchable rush of flying into the night, going from zero to 180 miles per hour in just under two seconds. The stakes are as high as they get: life and death. The shuttle (the large shoe-like fitting on the flight deck that eventually will slam my aircraft forward and into the air) makes a distinctive sound as it ratchets into place for the next launch—mine. The *click-click-click* kicks my already-elevated pulse into a steady lope. Giddyup, cowgirl.

It's so dark tonight that I can't even see the edge of the carrier's flight deck as I prepare for launch. The only thing keeping my ass (and the taxpayers' assets) from going over the edge is an attentive guy in a yellow shirt—my flight director—and a three-inch-tall scupper, or bumper. I know that if my aircraft does go over the edge of the flight deck, I probably won't make it out in time, since my ejection seat will be "out of the envelope"—meaning that I'm outside the area for safe operation of the ejection system. My chances of surviving if I "pushed the envelope" and tried to eject anyway? Not so good.

As the yellow shirt beckons my aircraft forward, my heart starts to race even faster. Sweat trickles down my back, and the nape of my neck tingles. I go through my memorized emergency procedures—my "boldface," as we aviators call it—one last time. Boldface procedures are those steps of an emergency procedure that must be performed immediately and without any reference to a written checklist.

Essentially, they are the first actions we must take in an emergency situation so we don't fall out of the sky.

For example, if one of my engines quits, I need to perform the following steps immediately (there's some aviation slang in here, but you'll get the drift):

SINGLE ENGINE FAILURE/CATAPULT LAUNCH

1. Set 10 degrees pitch attitude (14 units AOA maximum).
2. Rudder—opposite roll/yaw, supplemented by stick.
3. Both throttles—as required for positive rate of climb.
4. Landing gear—up.
5. Jettison—if required.

If we have a "cold cat shot"—that is, if the catapult doesn't work as advertised and I don't gain enough speed to launch successfully—I can (a) try to stop on the carrier deck; (b) jam the throttles into afterburner and attempt to get airborne anyway, though this is a tough call and not very likely to be successful (and punching a hole in the Pacific

Ocean with your fighter jet while going 200 miles per hour doesn't normally end well); or (c) eject from the aircraft. Right now, none of those seem like very fun options.

Now I'm running through the takeoff checklists, making sure that the trim is properly set (so in case my hand is forced off the control stick, the airplane will still fly properly—i.e., away from the water) and that I'm on "hot mic" for quick communications. My radar intercept officer (or RIO, my backseater) and I discuss the ejection envelope one last time. A great RIO is worth his or her weight in gold. Although the backseat does not have any flight controls, the RIO operates the radar systems, the missions system, and the complex cameras and targeting system, and monitors the hundreds of circuit breakers that control our intricate electrical systems. I follow the yellow shirt's signals closely and taxi slowly into place, splitting the catapult track with my nose tires.

It's almost show time. The final spotter looks like a third-base coach, arms flapping as he gives me the wings, flaps, and kneel signal and then, using just small head nods for lineup corrections, taxis me forward for final positioning on the catapult track. Several things happen almost simultaneously: I spread my wings for flight and drop my flaps. My RIO pulls a critical circuit breaker. And I drop the launch bar to lock into the shuttle that is about to propel me off the front end of the ship. Then the nose strut (part of the nose landing gear) compresses, and my jet is secured in place as the pressure from the catapult builds up. We lift our hands above the canopy rails for final checks so we don't inadvertently hit a flight control while the flight deck crew is under the fuselage of our jet. The "ordies"—ordnance men, outfitted in red shirts—make one last pass around the airplane, arming any missiles, bombs, or guns.

The catapult officer looks over each shoulder to make sure the catapult is clear, and on the run-up signal—two fingers held high overhead shaking back and forth—I'm off the brakes and quickly pushing the power up to "full military" (100 percent). My jet strains against the tension, ready to leap off the deck. I check my instruments and "wipe out" the controls, methodically hitting all corners—stick forward, stick aft, full right deflection, full left deflection—and then displacing full left and right rudder. If a flight control surface is caught on something or broken, we want to discover it now—not as we hurtle off the front end of the carrier attempting to get airborne!

Underneath the flight deck, last-second checks are made to the catapult system, ensuring that the right weight is set in the launch system and that all systems are a go.

After quickly confirming full flight control action and checking that all warning lights are out, I switch my lights on, indicating I am ready for launch. (In daylight, I would've given him a smart salute to show my readiness, but he'd never see it in the dark.)

The adrenaline blasts through my veins. For a few seconds, I will have no direct control. My fate will be in the hands of my teammates. I'll have to trust that the right weight was entered into the catapult launch system, that the maintenance on the jet is 4.0, and that everything else has been taken care of. I'll be relying on teamwork.

I lean slightly forward into my harness. Unlike pilots of other airplanes, who put their heads back against the headrest, I have to keep mine angled away. If I were to lean back into the headrest in the Tomcat during launch, I'd have whiplash for a week.

Suddenly we're moving. The airplane has a unique catapult shot trajectory on launch: It surges down before it lunges forward. After you've gained a little bit of experience, your butt can give you a decent indication of whether or not it's a "good" shot. But trusting your seat-of-the-pants feeling at night can be dangerous. In this E-ticket ride, better than any rollercoaster you could imagine, everything happens incredibly fast, I'm smashed into my seat from the g-forces accelerating us from zero to more than 180 miles per hour in just a couple seconds. My vision is a little blurry, and I strain to focus on good airspeed and good engines—the two things I'll need to safely fly away from the aircraft carrier.

Seconds later, we're in the night sky. Our airborne mission—or "hop"—has begun. Every mission is different, and the objectives are constantly changing; we may be performing night intercepts or night combat air patrol. But the first requirement is getting safely airborne. Let me tell you, there is no blacker emptiness than launching off the bow of the carrier with no stars, no moon, and no horizon.

Except, that is, for when you have to come back to the carrier and land.

The first time you ever attempt to qualify for aircraft carrier landings at night, you're in your combat fleet aircraft without a copilot or an instructor pilot, and there's no room for error. In the F-14 Tomcat, roughly 50 percent of naval aviators fail to pass on their first attempt to carrier qualify. At this advanced stage you normally get two chances to qualify. Fail to pass this critical screening on your second attempt, and your career as a naval aviator is likely over. You get bounced from your carrier-based squadron and may never fly in the Navy again. Clearly, there's a *little* bit of pressure.

United States Navy and Marine Corps carrier-based pilots are the only fighter and attack pilots *in the world* who land on aircraft carriers at night. No one else will even make the attempt. These landings are like controlled crashes. The touchdown is enough to destroy most other airplanes—but not the F-14.

Just seventy miles off the coast of Southern California, where I'm flying tonight, the Pacific Ocean provides some of the most treacherous swells and rollers found anywhere in the world. As I near the carrier and prepare to end my mission, I know that the deck is lurching up and down. I'm thinking about the first time I saw the propellers of an aircraft carrier exposed, up and out of the water. A hundred-thousand-ton aircraft carrier looked like a toy being tossed around in a bathtub. It was humbling, terrifying, amazing—another image that is forever burned in my memory.

I know that the spray of the ocean has made the deck slippery and treacherous; my carrier is plowing through ocean waves that are sometimes big enough to clear buildings. The whole thing is rocking and rolling, and there's no protection from the winds, which can approach upwards of 60 miles per hour. A senior officer once gave me a bit of pre-deployment advice: "When the deck is pitching, don't ever eat the chili mac before your night hop." (You can use your imagination to fill in the blanks.) And yet tonight I can't even see the deck, pitching or otherwise. But I know it's moving.

Your best bet in this situation is for a "pinky" recovery, meaning one at sunset, so you actually have a shot at just a tiny bit of discernible horizon, a slight distinction between sky and water, by which to orient yourself. No such luck tonight. The junior guy (or gal) doesn't get pinky landings often. Those are for the more seasoned, senior aviators.

Lucky dogs.

As I make my descent from the "Marshall stack" (the holding pattern where all the aircraft are tightly "stacked" at different altitudes),

I'm listening to three different radios with people all talking at once: my RIO, my wingman, and the ship. When I arrive to the stack, I fly a racetrack pattern at 300 knots: roughly two minutes in one direction, turn 180 degrees, and two minutes back. I'm constantly adjusting for the winds at altitude (either a headwind, a crosswind, or a tailwind) and the expected "push time"—the time that we need to hit, a certain window for arriving back at the ship on schedule. I'm watching my airspeed like a hawk and constantly scanning my instruments. A landing occurs every twenty-odd seconds on the aircraft carrier, and there's no room for error. None.

We are in radio contact with the *Lincoln,* and soon enough they give us directions: "One zero five, Marshal. Take angels seven. Your push time is one-five." This means we are to fly at seven thousand feet and need to be at a certain point in the sky to begin our approach at precisely fifteen minutes after the hour. My RIO calmly replies, "One zero five."

Throughout the constant communications, there is rarely even a hint of emotion. No panic, no stress, no anxiety. Nothing but cool, calm, collected confidence. Heart-rate monitors would tell a different story.

I hit my push time and start the descent toward the aircraft carrier. The *Lincoln* is on the move; the radio call comes out: "Ship's in a turn." Ugh. This does not make it easier. Not only is the deck pitching, but also now the ship is in a turn, moving away from me. Change is a constant.

As we roll onto the final bearing, I still can't see the ship when I get the call to extend my gear, hook, and flaps for landing: "One zero five dirty up."

"One zero five," calls my RIO coolly. I drop the gear, lower the flaps, and add a handful of power. We're getting close. My heart rate is increasing and my breathing slows down.

Still no sight of the carrier as radar control says, "Lock-on six miles. Call your needles." They want to confirm that our instruments are communicating with the ship and that we can see our glideslope and flight path. Sweat trickles down my back as I hear the aircraft ahead of me struggling to get aboard. I can hear on the radio that he bolters, meaning his tailhook—the steel hook below the jet—failed to engage the arresting wire that brings a thirty-ton aircraft to a stop, from more than 160 miles per hour to zero in 1.2 seconds. The ship gives him directions back to the night pattern. Now he gets to go back into the pitch dark and around for another attempt.

I can now see lights on the carrier—barely—but there's no hint of a horizon. The line of glowing points on the deck tilts side to side in a slow, seesaw motion. My runway is moving.

The countdown begins. At three quarters of a mile the landing signals officer pipes up: "One zero five, on and on, three quarters of a mile. Call the ball." My RIO answers, "One zero five, Tomcat ball, five-point-seven, Lohrenz."

I steel myself, letting my experience and practice stifle the fear in my stomach. I don't want to hit the water or the back end of the carrier—what we call a "ramp strike."

The LSO calmly replies, "Roger ball, Tomcat, wind is twenty knots." Inside the cockpit, my RIO is calling out our rate of descent in feet per minute: "Six hundred . . . six fifty . . . seven hundred . . . six fifty . . . six hundred . . . six hundred . . ." I'm focusing on three critical things: meatball, lineup, and angle of attack. Constantly shifting my focus at hyperspeed, hitting each of those things at nearly ten times a second. It takes extreme eye-hand coordination and focus-shifting ability, but if I can get all three of those things taken care of, it doesn't matter what else happens—we'll land safely. The concentration is intense. Life and death are in the balance.

Boom!

We hit the deck. I'm going 145 knots, nearly 170 miles per hour, when the arresting hook on my Tomcat snags a wire. I slam both throttles to full military and click my speedbrakes in, just in case my hook doesn't engage the arresting wire—or the wire snaps and I have to attempt to get flying again. My body is slammed forward with such force that it feels as if my arms and legs are going to separate from my body. I come to a full stop in 1.2 seconds.

Once I am positive that my aircraft has come to a halt, I pull the throttles back, reducing power to idle, and stay off the brakes. I simultaneously click off the external lights as my aircraft starts to roll back. The yellow shirt makes a clockwise windmill signal with his right hand, a signal for the arresting-gear crew to free me up. He quickly follows it with a right thumb to the palm of his left hand, signaling me to raise my tailhook immediately. I comply while also raising my flaps. I carefully follow the flight director to the right, aware of the slippery deck, and expeditiously exit the landing area. Another aircraft is only a few seconds behind me. Once I am out of the landing area, I reduce my taxi speed and pull my wings all the way back into the "oversweep" position—like tucking back bird wings—reducing the width of the wingspan and the amount of space the jet takes up on the flight deck.

And then it's over. I'm back aboard safely.

Nothing compares to that experience. And the only thing you can do to ever so slightly mitigate the tension and anxiety? Do it again. Over and over and over.

* * *

The cockpit of an F-14 is one of the most demanding environments on earth, and it's where I learned some of my most unforgettable lessons not just in flying, but also in life and in leadership. My journey to that cockpit—one that began when I decided to pursue a seemingly impossible dream that involved many challenges and trials—gave me indispensable insights as well. And my path after leaving the military, paved largely with my work among business leaders, from Fortune 500 executives to middle managers, has helped me further distill those lessons, share them with others, and then watch as leaders and their teams flourish.

In the years since I left the Navy and began working as a leadership consultant, I've been struck again and again by the parallels between the world of naval aviation and the world of business. In both, leaders must perform highly complex and high-pressure tasks in a constantly changing environment. People are counting on you to make the right moves. Mistakes can result in huge financial losses or damage to your career. But no parallel asserted itself more strongly or more consistently than this one: *High-performing teams require fearless leaders.*

This book is a call for each of us to lead more fearlessly—and a guide to show you how to get started. It's an encouragement to stand up and excel in the situations that would provoke fear in anyone, whether you're a newbie or a pro. It's an invitation to take the principles used by naval aviators to overcome tremendously demanding, stressful situations and apply them to your own leadership journey.

I've seen over and over how the skills necessary to effectively and inspiringly lead a team are lost when we're crippled by individual fears and perceived limitations. Maybe you have the opportunity to take on a leadership role but don't think of yourself as a leader. Maybe you're at the helm of a team now but don't feel respected or able to get things done. Maybe you have been leading for years and are simply looking for a way to do things better. Maybe you're so fearful of doing something wrong that you find yourself paralyzed, stuck in a rut, and embracing the status quo because it feels safe.

No matter your situation, the number one way to ensure that you're the best leader you can be is to build your ability to work through fear and do what needs to be done *in spite of* that fear. The best leaders stare fear, uncertainty, and discomfort in the face. They push themselves out of their comfort zones. They aren't content to rest on their laurels—ever. And they don't make excuses about why they can't take the next step forward on their leadership journey. They go in, knowing that anything great they want to accomplish *will* involve fear and discomfort, and they decide to go for it anyway. With every opportunity they take to stare fear in the face, they become stronger, more courageous, and more confident.

The ability to work through fear kept me alive as I operated under dangerous conditions and in life-or-death situations on the flight deck of that aircraft carrier, and it's what keeps any leader relevant, respected, and moving forward. If you're able to shape the fear into something useful, you'll be unstoppable. Letting fear be your copilot is a fundamental element of the art of leading well.

But just because this book is about fearlessness, don't think it's intended only as a remedial work for shrinking violets. Even if you're doing leadership right, you *will* feel fear, no matter how big and bad you are. Fearless leadership isn't just about dealing with trepidation and anxiety when they come up; it's also about seeking out new fears to overcome, because you know that doing so will make you a better leader.

You also don't have to be interested in the military to enjoy and benefit from this book. You don't have to want to fly a fighter jet. You don't have to want to be a pioneer of any sort. But you do have to be interested in reaching peak performance as a leader, whatever that means for you.

Average leaders are everywhere, many of them well intentioned and basically competent. But this book isn't for those who want to land a spot in a comfortable office and hang out there for decades. This book is for people who want to step up their game and move to the next level, whether that means taking on your very first leadership position, pushing for that promotion into the C-suite, or revolutionizing your approach to being CEO. Through the tools and approaches covered in the pages of this book, I hope to challenge, inform, and inspire your team to move fearlessly to higher levels of performance.

In part I, we're going to break down the three fundamental traits that every fearless leader has: courage (chapter 1), tenacity (chapter 2), and integrity (chapter 3). These three are the "secret sauce" for leading any team through constant change and challenging times, and we'll explore how you can strengthen them in yourself. We'll also see how these traits work in real life, through stories of my transformation from a regular Midwestern girl to the US Navy's first female F-14 Tomcat fighter pilot, and through examples of leaders in the business world. These chapters will help you grow confident and gain the tools you'll need to lead yourself down the right path—a vital skill to acquire before you attempt to lead others. When I strapped into that fighter cockpit and the canopy snapped shut, I was the one at the controls—alone. Relying on courage, tenacity, and integrity, I had to be able to lead myself well and make great decisions while traveling at the speed of sound. You'll increase your ability to do the same as we discuss these three fundamental traits.

In part II, we'll turn outward and dive into the nitty-gritty of what fearless leadership looks like in action. You'll discover

- how to set a clear vision that will inspire and align your team (chapter 4);
- how to create awareness of a shared culture and get your people working as a team, all rowing in the same direction (chapter 5);
- how to adapt the military's process to your own team and use it to prepare, perform, and prevail in a constantly changing world (chapter 6); and, last but definitely not least,
- how to be resilient so you can bounce back when bad stuff happens—and actually benefit from the experience (chapter 7).

We all have an instinctive need to be part of something bigger than ourselves—a family, a sports team, a corporation, a community—and each of these units requires fearless leaders if it's going to flourish. There's nothing stopping you from being one of them. If you follow the lessons laid out in the following chapters and integrate them in small, steady ways in your daily life, you'll witness your leadership ability growing stronger and stronger. I've seen it work firsthand.

Just like flying an F-14, leading fearlessly never gets easy, and it requires nerves of steel. But I firmly believe that absolutely anyone can build his or her leadership skills and reap the rewards of doing so. Let's move on to chapter 1 and see why a fearless leadership role is possible for you—provided you have the courage to step up and take it.

PART I: FUNDAMENTALS OF FEARLESS LEADERSHIP

Chapter 1

COURAGE

SUMMONING THE BRAVERY TO FLY HIGH

The future belongs to those who believe in the beauty of their dreams.
—Eleanor Roosevelt

I knew from the very beginning that I'd be an aviator. Flying was in my blood.

My older brother and I grew up playing with Dad's silk maps and flight gear from Vietnam. We'd perform imaginary feats of daring and skill, pretending to be pilots just like our dad, a former United States Marine Corps aviator. After he left the armed forces, my dad flew for a major airline until retirement; my mom had been a flight attendant before having us kids. Given this heritage, my brother and I had no doubt even as kids that we were destined for the cockpit—and we were both right.

The path to a piloting career is a challenge for anyone, no matter how driven and naturally skilled you may be. What I didn't know as a child, though, was that it would require an extra helping of courage from me, simply because I was a girl. On top of that, I decided while an undergrad at the University of Wisconsin–Madison that I didn't just want to be any ol' pilot. I wanted to be a naval aviator—a coveted title even among men in the field. For a woman, especially in the 1990s, aiming for that goal seemed almost silly. Nevertheless, it's what I wanted. I was very quiet about my aspirations. My family and my roommates knew, but that was it. I told no one else. I held this dream tightly to my chest like a guarded secret. I knew to many it would sound like a crazy idea. I didn't want their doubt to taint my dream.

The first step anyone has to take on the path to naval aviation is getting commissioned as a naval officer. For me, the best way to do that was to apply to Aviation Officer Candidate School (AOCS) at the Naval Air Station in Pensacola, Florida. Highly selective and intensely competitive, this fourteen-week training program is for potential naval aviators, naval flight officers, a handful of aviation maintenance duty officers, and intelligence officers. If I were accepted, AOCS would do its best to convert me, in less than four months, from a run-of-the-mill college graduate to a naval officer.

But first, I had to get in. My brother had done it successfully, and his example encouraged me. Still, the AOCS application process was intimidating. With no flying experience under my belt, I applied for AOCS in the summer of 1990. I wasn't an aerospace engineering major; I had earned my BA with a double major in psychology and social work. I wasn't sure how I was going to do on the initial entry exams. The tests would include math skills, reading skills, mechanical comprehension, spatial apperception, and aviation and nautical information. I was pretty sure that as long as I was prepared and went through the study guides, I would be okay—but there were no guarantees. Pensacola's AOCS is the place where legends were made—people like Neil Armstrong, Buzz Aldrin, John McCain. The Navy wants only the best of the best. I knew that even if I got in, only a handful of those who made it to Pensacola would earn those prized aviator wings. Only an extremely small percentage of student naval aviators go on to become aircraft carrier fighter pilots.

Right around the time I was graduating from college and getting ready to apply, my brother was graduating from AOCS himself. In May 1990 I went down to Pensacola for his graduation and got to meet all of his new friends, aviation officer candidates like him. One night a bunch of us all went out to the Flora-Bama, a legendary beach bar on the Alabama-Florida state line. Naturally, after a few beers, conversation started flowing. I'd been cast in the role of "little sister," and questions flew when these new officers discovered that I too wanted to fly. Most of the guys were supportive and thought it was "cool." Some thought I was bat-shit crazy; several of them said things like, "You seem way too nice. Why would you want to do this?" But one guy at the Flora-Bama that night was vehemently opposed to the idea of me becoming a naval aviator.

This was the first time I'd run across somebody my age who truly didn't believe women should be in combat. This new adversary of mine was passionate about his position; he proclaimed that women should be the keepers of the home and family and had no business being in combat. I was shocked. This guy was well spoken and college educated, a friend of my own brother—how on earth could he be such a caveman?

With his statements, the lines in the sand were drawn. We both argued our positions, nearly shouting over the bar noise, and by the end of the night we had to just agree to disagree on this one point. He was a sweet Southern boy from Louisiana—pure Cajun. His were long-held, ultra-traditional views. I could respect that, and I probably wasn't going to change his opinion.

But the bluntness of that opinion left me stunned. How could somebody who didn't even know me or know whether I would be capable of being a naval aviator say, right out of the gate, "You don't belong here"? To me, that just seemed crazy. And it was a little scary, too.

After all, I wanted to serve my country, just like this guy did. I was drawn to naval aviation and the culture it held so dear—mission before self, a warrior mentality—just like this guy was. I knew the program would be hard enough on its own, but now I had to face the truth: I would have to fight some people on the inside. If the people whom I was supposed to be working *with* were actually against the idea of me even being there, would it be impossible to make it through the program? Would I have the strength to express my convictions when challenged?

This guy wasn't the first to give me flak—far from it. But as I began to take steps toward my dream of naval aviation, I started to realize that certain parts of this process would be much harder than I had ever imagined.

Courage: The First Element of Fearless Leadership

I tell you this story because these feelings are common to anyone who has accepted the challenge of leadership. After years of coaching leaders and businesspeople, I've seen the same self-doubt plague those who face their first leadership role or a step up into a larger, more challenging role. If leaders aren't able to shove that hesitancy to the side and be bold in their convictions, things usually don't go well.

Courage—because it is the flip side of fear—is the first vital element of fearless leadership. If you can cultivate courage in yourself, you'll have what it takes to see the limitless possibilities for your future, tamp down the voices telling you what you can't do it (whether they're internal or external), and come into your own as a fearless leader.

To some degree, all leaders, even the pros, have that knot in their stomach: *What if people don't like what I have to say?* But courage often involves the display of candor: being willing to have the tough conversations, to give hard feedback. Courage can mean speaking up even when you know the existing culture won't support you. Courage also means admitting when you were wrong and holding yourself accountable. Leaders who don't display courage—fearful leaders—discourage conflicting opinions and squash dissent. Weak executives say what their boss expects them to. You know who they are: the "Yes, sir" and "Yes, ma'am" folks—the ones who give in to pressure and then walk away rolling their eyes.

Having the courage to take the first step on the leadership journey is never easy, but if you don't do it, you're bound to miss out on becoming the leader you could have been. If I hadn't had the courage to apply to AOCS—and then keep pushing until I was holding the stick of an F-14—I would've missed out on serving my country *and* flying the amazing airplane I was so passionate about. That's a high price to pay for the comfort of giving in.

Just as it took courage to walk down that flight line full of F-14 Tomcats, where others did not dare to go, it takes serious day-to-day courage to lead in a professional sense. Leadership requires the ability to confidently articulate your message and the willingness, on occasion, to say—and do—the unpopular. Courageous leaders have to be able to work through difficult situations and accept both responsibility and personal accountability for the outcomes of their decisions. True bravery in leadership revolves around your ability to summon the courage to regard yourself as a leader and then maintain that courage in the day-to-day guiding of your team. Pursuing your desire to lead even when everyone else, including the voice in your head, is saying you can't do it—*that's* courage.

The topic of courage doesn't receive enough attention, in my opinion. Contrary to what many people think, courage does not consist of the absence of fear. Courage, rather, is the mastering of that fear: feeling the fear and going forward anyway. Courage means that you keep going even when the going gets really, really tough. It's the inner fortitude that allows you to face danger, to overcome barriers, and to step up and take a chance—even when a situation seems impossible, even when you're terrified. This is not the same thing as taking bad risks or showing false bravado. It is simply choosing to live with the possibility of hope instead of being crushed and paralyzed by your fears. The most successful people I know have that kind of courage, that kind of bravery that makes other people scratch their heads and say, "I can't believe you did that!"

Courage is starting another business even when you failed the first time—or getting right back in the cockpit when one of your best friends is killed.

Then doing it again when another is killed.

Then again . . .

And again . . .

That's a picture of true courage: recognizing the risk of doing the right thing, and then going forward. A hero isn't someone who doesn't feel fear; it's someone who feels the fear and does it anyway.

FEEL THE FEAR, AND DO IT ANYWAY!

Feel the fear, and do it anyway!

When leaders display courage,

whether in the air or in the boardroom, it's truly contagious. That's why troops will charge a heavily fortified hill or follow a courageous leader into some other seemingly impossible situation. Everyone has fears. Fighter pilots do. Navy SEALs do. Army Rangers do. And CEOs do. Those who succeed look fear in the eye, accept it, and decide to be courageous anyway.

The question is, how can *you* foster the courage it takes to lead?

Develop a "Why *Not* Me?" Attitude

The first step in any leader's journey is accepting the fact that he or she is worthy of being a leader. Pursuing leadership is highly a personal decision, and I've seen many people back away from great leadership opportunities, spouting lines like "I'm not sure I'm ready" and "I just think it's too soon" and "I still have some growing to do." These statements, though masquerading as neutral, are actually negative. They almost always mask insecurity and a desire to avoid the challenges that come with leadership. These statements are the fear talking—and it's saying self-defeating things. You take them to heart, but you would never dream of saying such things to anyone else! Nine times out of ten, the fear is telling you a bullshit story—yet you believe it.

> **NINE TIMES OUT OF TEN, THE FEAR IS TELLING YOU A BULLSHIT STORY— YET YOU BELIEVE IT.**

Everyone has his or her own personal self-doubts and fears to face. But to be a fearless leader, you must recognize your own value. Dharmesh Shah, cofounder and chief technology officer of HubSpot, believes that one of the qualities of truly confident people is their inclination to think, "Why not me?" rather than sit on their hands and wait for an opportunity that never comes.[1] I heartily agree. Why *not* you? When you're telling yourself or others that you're just not sure or not ready yet, you're shutting yourself out of a world of limitless possibilities. Instead, when you consider an opportunity—even one that comes with challenges—ask yourself, "Why *not* me?"

Every good idea started off with a question: "I wonder if . . .?" By its very nature, this question comes with the potential for both success and failure—and you have to be willing to find out which outcome triumphs. History shows that we need to keep looking around the corner, to keep pushing the envelope, to grow into the person we were meant to be. This isn't about finding the perfect job or making enough money; it's about realizing your potential and seeking your passion in life. Sadly, most people talk themselves out of their dreams and into mediocrity. Self-doubt kills more dreams than failure ever will.

As I prepared for Aviation Officer Candidate School, a parade of negative thoughts marched through my head: *What if I'm not smart enough? Do I have what it takes to do this? Am I good enough? What if I fail? What if I'm not ready?* If I'd nurtured them, letting them drop anchor in my psyche and completely take over, I would never have had the guts to fill out that first application. Or to take the Armed Services Vocational Aptitude Battery (ASVAB—the test that all enlistees have to pass before joining the armed forces). Or to make it through the first day of AOCS. Because each of those things presented roadblocks, challenges, and the opportunity to fail. And if I'd decided to wait until someone invited me to be a female fighter pilot—well, I'd still be waiting. Someone else would've gotten there first. Someone else would be living my dream.

It's likely that you've already displayed courage to get where you are now, but with every step up, a new level of courage is required. When I decided to go for AOCS, an outside observer might've thought I pretty much had it together. No self-doubt at all, right? After all, I was a three-time varsity letter winner on the nationally ranked, über-competitive rowing team at the University of Wisconsin. I had done pre-Olympic training. I *knew* I could perform, and I had— at peak levels. Yet even with my academic pedigree and competitive sports background, I wondered if I would be good enough.

The prospect of failing is never fun, and more often than not we choose not to risk failing, not to risk being vulnerable or finding out we're not good enough. But what kind of a life is that?

So, this is the first step you must take as a leader: Summon the courage to know that you *can* be a leader. No one but you can give you permission to lead. The truth is that we're all scared some of the time. The people who *do* succeed in leadership are the ones who believe they're just as worthy of a leadership role as the next guy. They think, "Why *not* me?"

I'll say it again and again: You *can* start from where you are with what you've got and go where you want to go. All it takes is the courage to step up and take the opportunity when it comes along. Remember to ask, "Why *not* me?" when you feel that doubt creeping back. This will encourage you to venture forward and be confident, despite the gremlins you might face along the way.

Acknowledge That Leadership Isn't a "Gift"

Leadership skills are for everyone—including you. Leadership isn't an innate "gift." It might come more naturally to some, but we're all leaders in some capacity. No matter what our roles are in life, we all engage in leadership and teamwork every day.

If you're uncertain whether you have what it takes to step up and take on a more formal leadership role, stop doubting. You *do* have what it takes. But you have to believe it and be confident in it. You may be a leadership newbie—a "nugget," as we aviators would say—but you have what it takes to become a "centurion," an expert.

On the other hand, one of the best ways to kill your potential as a leader is to get stuck on the idea that leadership ability is an inborn talent—something that some of us have and others don't. If you go and ask somebody whether great leaders are born or made, you won't find too many people who say that leadership is purely innate. Most will tell you that it's a mix, with more emphasis on the "made" side. Research supports that idea, with one study of genetic twins concluding that only about 30 percent of leadership-role occupancy comes down to genetic factors.[2]

I think we should toss out even that figure. Yes, certain hardwired personality traits, like extroversion, can help a person lead well. But if you focus on that idea, you give your subconscious mind a great excuse to back down in the face of fear. You give it an easy out, a default answer to "Why not me?" Your challenge is figuring out what you need to do to become the most effective leader you can be, no matter what your strengths are or are not—even if you're introverted, even if you don't like confrontation, even if you're not naturally aggressive and forceful. Leadership skills are for anyone who has a passion for achieving excellence and helping others do the same. You just have to find the courage to truly believe that you can do it.

Some women especially may face an obstacle in this regard. Jody Detjen, coauthor of *The Orange Line: A Woman's Guide to Integrating Career, Family, and Life*, said, "Women often choose to stay in individual contributor roles because they think they're not ready, or they accept the role and find it's too much work because they take on everyone else's. Once they were willing to ask for help and support, they learned to delegate and trust their own abilities."[3]

A study done by the Hay Group supports this idea. According to *Harvard Business Review,* the study found that women tend to be "less deliberate than men in their career progressions," focusing on building skills and learning rather than creating opportunities for themselves on the path to a specific position.[4] The research found that many women feel they played a somewhat passive role in their career advancement, allowing things to happen to them rather than going out and grabbing what they wanted. They also hesitated more when offered promotions, in part because they didn't expect them or felt unprepared for the role.

Male or female, stepping up and taking ownership of your leadership career takes courage, but if you shirk opportunities out of worry that you're not cut out for a certain role, you are unquestionably passing up chances to grow into a fearless leader.

Stop Flying under the Radar

How can you tell when to stand up or stand out? In a US study on conformity to feminine norms, researchers uncovered what women associate as the most important attributes of femininity.[5] These include being friendly and nice in relationships, pursuing a thin body ideal, refraining from calling attention to one's talents or abilities (modesty), maintaining the home (domesticity), caring for children, investing in romantic relationships, sexual fidelity, and using one's own resources to invest in one's personal appearance. The ideal of taking on a leadership role is nowhere in the list.

It's important to understand why this matters. All of this means that in order to conform, women need to be willing to play a small game and avoid rocking the boat. We're expected not to assert ourselves, not to carry around an extra ten pounds, and certainly not to tell people we are kicking ass in our jobs.

But playing small serves *nobody*.

This is a daily struggle for those women I know who are currently climbing the ladder—and even for those who have made it to the top. That being said, trying to fit in or fly under the radar can negatively affect men just as easily.

When I was in the military, I certainly tried not to draw any extra attention to myself. This was challenging enough as a woman who is almost six feet tall. But I didn't even do the standard flight line photo shoots.

PLAYING SMALL SERVES *NOBODY*.

Not sure what I mean by this? If you've ever been inside any former military aviator's home, chances are you've seen the "I love me" wall: a space adorned with pictures of the aviator in front of just about every airplane the individual ever flew—or walked by.

I don't think there is anything wrong with that. But you may be surprised to know that most of the women aviators I know don't have nearly as many photos. I only have a couple. Even though I was more than willing to be behind the camera, taking lots of pictures of my friends in front of airplanes, I was always hesitant to be the one getting my picture taken. I didn't want to look like I was showing off.

It doesn't make much sense, looking back on it, and it certainly is one of my regrets. But the truth is, women still battle this issue in the corporate world—playing small, trying to blend in, making nice, flying under the radar. Are these norms outdated, obsolete, or irrelevant? Unfortunately, no.

I was at dinner with a client—a global Fortune 50 company—and a team of about thirty-five people when one of the most senior women executives stood up to leave. As she was walking out the door, she stopped by the table where I was seated, put her hand on my shoulder, and said, "So why are you here? I don't understand. Your husband works, right? And you have kids? So why are you here? You should be at home."

I sat there dumbfounded as my cheeks turned hot, not exactly sure what to say. With my mom's Southern saying, "Bless your heart," running through my head, I tried to sweetly tell this senior executive how I was here to help her team become better leaders. Her response was, "I still don't understand why you would be here. Your husband works."

So the norms are still the norms, and standing up and speaking out is what is required. Knowing your value, speaking up, and not flying under the radar—this is what fearless leadership is about.

Banish Your Limiting Beliefs

Almost everything about our self-belief—how much we believe we can achieve—we learn early on in life. These limiting beliefs shape everything we do. Our own perspective on our ability to change or to effect a different outcome is profound. Some of us are born with more self-belief than others or raised to believe in ourselves to a greater degree. But we all perform based on what we *believe* we can do, not based on what we actually can do.

All of us (except for the total narcissists) deal with lies told by our limiting beliefs. And those little liars get embedded into our subconscious, stealing our courage and stopping us dead in our tracks. The negative and lasting impacts are real, and they shackle our growth.

They impact our ability to achieve and our perception of what is possible. We respond automatically, the only safe way we know how: We play it conservative and small, and we go with only those efforts that seem certain to succeed. When these limiting beliefs hold sway and hold us hostage, we don't reach our full potential.

WHETHER YOU THINK YOU CAN, OR YOU THINK YOU CAN'T, YOU'RE RIGHT.

—HENRY FORD

Unfortunately, we usually accept these limiting beliefs without identifying, challenging, or questioning them. They often harden into assumptions that shape our realities. But these fears are paper tigers—they have no teeth. If you get stuck on the idea that maybe you just weren't born with a special knack for leadership, someone else will seize your opportunity while you're making excuses. Instead, you must see challenges as exciting opportunities rather than discouraging obstacles. As successful investor and entrepreneur Mark Cuban advises, "Always wake up with a smile, knowing that today you are going to have fun accomplishing what others are too afraid to do."

A resounding *belief* that you can grow and develop your abilities actually improves your performance and profoundly affects the way you lead—and the way you live your life. The research of Carol Dweck, a Stanford psychology professor and leading researcher on mindset and belief systems, supports the notion that if you simply believe that you can become a better leader, you increase your chances of improving your leadership skills.

How can this be? Dweck's research indicates that there are two basic mindsets: the fixed mindset and the growth mindset. These mindsets determine how a person judges his or her own abilities, talents, potential, and intelligence. If you have a fixed mindset, you believe that your qualities are carved in stone; they are, well, fixed. In this thinking, you are stuck with whatever intelligence, creative abilities, or personality traits you have now.

Dweck's research shows that with a fixed mindset, you tend to fear challenges. Why? Because for fixed-mindset people, setbacks are catastrophic. After all, if who you are is so tightly linked with a small category of things you are good at, then failure attacks the core of your identity. Failing at something, to people with a fixed mindset, means *you* are a failure. Such individuals hold the belief that trying and failing is worse than not trying at all. The fixed mindset can stop us from trying and taking risks, simply because we don't have the courage to fail.

The growth mindset, on the other hand, comes from the belief that you can develop and strengthen your basic qualities through effort and constant learning. This mindset recognizes that yes, people are different, but everyone can improve with effort and grow their talents, abilities, and even intelligence through application and experience. The hallmark quality of the growth mindset, according to Dweck, is "the passion for stretching yourself and sticking to it, even (or especially) when it's not going well . . . This is the mindset that allows people to thrive during some of the most challenging times in their lives."[6]

Smart people succeed, says the fixed mindset. Therefore, if you succeed, you're a smart person. Conversely, people who don't succeed must not be smart. Given these assumptions, it makes sense to pick the easier problem so that success is more likely and thus you validate your smartness. Pick a hard problem and you may fail, revealing your stupidity.

People can get smarter, says the growth mindset, encouraging them to do so by stretching themselves and taking on challenges. Therefore, the growth mindset picks the hard problem. Who cares if you fail? You'll learn something that will help you succeed next time!

Understanding your mindset and how it drives your limiting beliefs—and therefore, your potential—is critical. How can we change our orientation from a fixed mindset to a growth or learning mindset? Simply by choosing to make that change. Just by knowing about the two mindsets, you can start thinking and reacting in new ways. We actually get to choose how we think about setbacks. Instead of automatically throwing up our hands at the first signs of defeat or resistance, we can choose to make the effort to determine our success.

WE ACTUALLY GET TO CHOOSE HOW WE THINK ABOUT SETBACKS.

Vince Lombardi famously said, "Perfection is not attainable, but if we chase perfection, we can catch excellence." If we raise our belief levels—feeling free to chase perfection but knowing that we'll fall short—this will carry us in an upward spiral on the path of continuous improvement.

Get Comfortable with Being Uncomfortable

Courage isn't comfortable. Courage means breaking *out* of your comfort zone. Leading fearlessly forces us to confront uncertainty, doubt, and the possibility of failure, and that's rarely a fun experience in the moment. Our natural inclination is to shirk discomfort. After all, life seems easier when you're not pushing the envelope, when you're not taking chances. But no one will stand up for a wimpy leader. No one will respect or follow someone who's unwilling to make the tough calls. That's why courage is the cornerstone of effective, fearless leadership.

But you can't simply call on courage when it's convenient for you. Courage is like a muscle; it needs to be exercised every day. You can exercise it and make it strong, but you have to be willing to take that first step and keep going from there.

Get in the arena. Take the initiative and take action. Fearless leaders do this. If you don't boldly take the first step, whether it's acting with confidence in your team or accepting the challenge to speak the unpopular truth, *how on earth* can you ever expect the people you lead to do the same?

COURAGE MEANS BREAKING *OUT* OF YOUR COMFORT ZONE.

Fearless leadership requires you to embrace discomfort—to get comfortable being uncomfortable. As Dropbox CEO Drew Houston said in a commencement address to MIT's graduating class, "Your biggest risk isn't failing, it's being too comfortable."[7] If you're not ready to push off the coziness of the status quo, you're not going to go far.

Would it have been more comfy for me to choose a career path that didn't pit me against tradition and a whole swath of people? Would it have been easier to avoid challenging those who didn't get why a girl would want to be a fighter pilot or, worse, who felt that a woman in combat was wrong? Sure! You bet! But for better or worse, naval aviation is what I felt called to do. If you feel the same call to leadership, you can't let the siren call of something easier lure you away from your target. You must not only endure that discomfort, but relish it. When you do, you'll be in the company of the best leaders.

The experiences that get you out of your comfort zone are the ones that will make the difference in your leadership career. The uncomfortable experiences—the ones you *think* you're not ready for, the ones that leave you with a little vurp in your throat or a knot in your stomach—are the experiences that will help you grow the most in the long run.

Leadership consultant and coauthor of *Strengths Based Leadership* Barry Conchie says that high-potential managers and leaders need *additive experiences.*[8] An additive experience could be running a risky project, integrating a complex acquisition, being promoted to a high-visibility position, navigating extreme cultural diversity, or leading a newly formed, cross-functional team. If you want to improve your leadership skills—if you want to become a top leader—you must integrate these tough assignments into your career plans. You will never know what you are capable of until you've pushed yourself past that point of what you thought was possible!

Ultimately, we should not shy away from but savor those moments when we can display courage and push out of our comfort zones. Those times might provoke fear, but as author Susan Jeffers says, "Pushing through fear is less frightening than living with the bigger underlying fear that comes from a feeling of helplessness."[9] One of my fears is that I might look back on my life and wonder what I did with it. I don't want to be sitting around at eighty thinking, *If only I would've . . . .*

If we don't get comfortable being uncomfortable, our lives will be filled with regrets and *coulda-shoulda-wouldas.* None of us knows just how good we can be, but each day we get the opportunity to push ourselves beyond yesterday's level, to smash through those limiting beliefs—those barriers that hold us back.

Take No Notice of Naysayers

My dad used to say that people who tell you that you can't succeed are the ones who don't want you to succeed. It's true. On your leadership journey, there are going to be a lot of people who try to impede your success, whether in small, subtle ways or in more obvious ones. Leading requires that you not only push through your own limiting barriers, but also push through the fear of what other people think about you. Stop worrying about how they're going to react once you step outside the box they put you in. When people tell you that you can't do something, learn to respond, "Just watch me!"

While following the path I chose for my life, I've experienced a lot of unsupportive comments. I let the overwhelming majority of them roll off my back—not always an easy thing to do, especially when the comments are personal. But just when I think I've heard every offensive remark, another one pops up. It takes courage to repel this negative commentary, whether it's subtle or outlandish, and keep going toward your goal. And it doesn't matter whether you're a man or a woman, young or old, seasoned or wet behind the ears—if you're pushing for greatness, you *will* be the target of naysaying. The conversation I had that night at the Flora-Bama, with the newly minted officer who thought I should stay out of AOCS, tweaked that little part of me that said, "Really? You don't think I can do this? Well, I'm going to do everything in my power to show you you're wrong!"

Maybe that sounds a little contrarian, but I prefer to think of it as optimistic. Trying to fly under the radar and avoid offending anybody can be challenging. If you don't stick up for yourself, who will? Plus, committing to prove your naysayers wrong is a great way to turn their negativity into fuel. People with negative energy might try to stand in your way, but nobody can actually prevent you from stepping into your role as a leader—except you, if you listen to them. Learn to distinguish between the people who succeed *because of* and the people who succeed *in spite of.* You *always* have a choice—you can choose to be bold and step up. It all comes down to whether you choose to tune out the naysayers, feel the fear, and go for it anyway.

People will tell you to give up. They'll say you aren't cut out for "this kind of work." But so what if they think so? Why should their opinion change anything? This is *your* life, *your* path. These are *your* dreams. There will be bumps in the road, but there will also be awesome, unforeseen opportunities. And more often than not, as my dad used to say, "Those who tell you 'You can't' and 'You won't' are probably the ones most scared that you will."

YOU *ALWAYS* HAVE A CHOICE—YOU CAN CHOOSE TO BE BOLD AND STEP UP.

We hear all these little messages and negative labels from naysayers, starting at an early age: You're not smart enough. You're too slow. Too young. Too old. Too inexperienced. Too overqualified. Too broke. Too fat. Too thin. Too quiet. Too assertive. Too different. Too whatever. And these discouragements don't always come from evil people who want to see us fail. Quite often, they come from people who love us and care about us—parents, family, friends, peers, coworkers, teammates, teachers, or doctors. Sometimes they have good intentions; they don't want to see us hurt or disappointed when faced with a challenging reality. So they try to lower our expectations.

In my case, the naysaying started very early on—at birth. When I came into the world, my hips weren't fully formed, and it wasn't until I was about six weeks old that the doctors realized this. The prognosis was grim. My parents were told over and over again I would never be able to walk and that I would probably be confined to a wheelchair for the rest of my life. *She won't be capable. Just learn to accept it. Sorry.*

It was devastating for my parents, naturally. But once they regrouped, they sought out second, third, and fourth opinions. After finding a surgeon who looked at my case a little differently, they had a glimmer of hope. I underwent surgery and was plastered into a full-blown, half-body cast for almost the first two years of my life. That plaster abomination held my hips and legs in a frog-like position as my bones were coaxed into growing into the proper position. And it weighed a ton, getting heavier as I grew.

There were still no guarantees that I would ever be capable of walking, and the doctors continued to tell my parents to expect the worst. One particular family photo, of me with my grandma, is striking. The pained expression on her face shares a lot. She clearly didn't believe that this cast was going to work, and believing that I would never be ambulatory, I think, was painful for her.

As I grew out of the casting phase, I had the joy of wearing white leather boots that were clamped into a red metal bar. This rudimentary torture device would lock my feet into position, pointed 180 degrees out from each other, keeping my hips stable—while still not allowing me to walk. My dad would always tell me that they knew exactly when I woke up, because they would hear a *thunk!* as I dropped out of bed and dragged my way into their room, determined to say, "Good morning." One of the few times that I ever saw my dad cry was when he would talk about this.

Still, no one thought I would be strong enough to walk.

Eventually the time came to try. Step by determined step, it happened. In spite of the belief of everyone but my parents that it *would never happen*—that I was not capable, I was a lost cause, my fate was sealed, I'd never be strong enough, I might as well move on with my life—it happened.

I'll never run a seven-minute mile, and to this day, when I get really tired, my left foot will point in a little bit. But I proved wrong all those who were so sure I wouldn't walk.

Tell me I can't do something? Ha! Just watch me.

If you adopt this optimistic attitude, you'll be unstoppable. It will help you not only step up to the challenge of leadership, but also display courage again and again in the decisions you make as a leader. Consider what Southwest Airlines CEO James Parker did following the devastating events of September 11, 2001. Bucking the aviation industry's job-slashing trend, he courageously announced that he would keep all employees and even continue a profit-sharing program for them. To resist doing what everyone else in the industry was doing, *plus* go a step further? That takes courage. It takes an ability to tune out the negative chatter that Parker certainly heard when he announced such a bold move. I'm certain you can do the same.

* * *

Ultimately, fearless leadership demands that you *choose* to be courageous. That you choose excellence. That you choose to look fear in the face. The world is not a place for average anymore—not if you want to succeed in your job and in your life. If you're passionate about leading, you can't be afraid to put yourself out there and tap into the limitless possibilities around you. In other words, you have to display courage, the first element of fearless leadership.

The absence of courage stunts our growth, narrows our ambitions, and kills our dreams. The notion that only a few extraordinary people at the top of an organization can provide all the leadership needed today is ridiculous. If you're interested in leading, go for it. Don't second-guess or look for validation. Instead, look for ways you can lead today so you can reach greater levels of leadership tomorrow. March forward courageously into your future. Being courageous is a choice, one that each of us has the capacity to make.

Motivational leader and founder of *SUCCESS* magazine Darren Hardy once said, "You only need to be courageous for twenty seconds at a time." This is a relief to those of us who don't feel brave or courageous twenty-four hours a day, seven days a week. Which is probably all of us, by the way (unless you're Batman).

So, mathematically, that means we don't have to be courageous 99.9305556 percent of the time. Seems doable, don't you think? Twenty seconds of courage at a time? We all should be able to manage that. You just need to make a habit of demonstrating short, consistent bursts of fearlessness when and where it matters.

Acts of bravery don't always take place in the cockpit at Mach 2. They can take place on otherwise normal days, in the moments when you have the courage to honor your voice, your instincts, and your passions as a leader.

Chapter 2

TENACITY

STICKING TO IT, EVEN WHEN IT'S HARD

Nothing in the world can take the place of persistence.
Talent will not; nothing is more common than unsuccessful
men with talent. Genius will not; unrewarded genius is almost a
proverb. Education will not; the world is full of educated derelicts.
Persistence and determination alone are omnipotent.
—Calvin Coolidge

"Is the machine on?" I asked the woman.

She gave me a surprised look. "Hmm," she replied. "Yes, it is."

I kept staring at the screen display in front of me. It showed several rows of tiny rings against a white background, like Cheerios on a blank sheet of paper. The woman, a petty officer who was administering my vision exam, had asked me to take a look at the top row and tell her which Cheerio seemed to be closest. Feeling mildly panicked, I realized none of them looked close to me. As far as my eyes were concerned, they were all exactly the same distance away.

"Ah, well. Looks like you don't have any depth perception," the petty officer said, scratching pen against clipboard. "That's not a big deal. You can always do something else, like be a nurse."

This lady *had* to be kidding me. This was midsummer 1990. I'd been up since 0400 that morning, taking a never-ending battery of physical exams that would qualify me for admission to Aviation Officer Candidate School in Pensacola, the first stop on my path to becoming a naval aviator. Now it was late afternoon, and this woman was telling me, quite nonchalantly, that my dream was over before it even started. And these were only the regional-level exams. I had yet to pass the Naval Aviation Entrance Physical Evaluation (NAEPE) down at Pensacola—another prerequisite for entry into AOCS.

I left that exam room stunned. Like any young person, I'd had my eyes tested a bunch of times and was never told I didn't have depth perception. And yet now I had this giant red flag on my record, and it meant I couldn't fly. It didn't matter how qualified I was in every other area; according to that one little red stamp, I was done.

But something was stirring in me, and I knew I would not be deterred by this one moment. The way I look at it is, should I stop the first time someone tells me no? I don't think so.

For the next month, I went to several other Navy- and Air Force–sanctioned optometrists and ophthalmologists and had my eyes retested, hoping to prove that indeed I *did* have depth perception and that it was well within naval regulations. I was right. My eyes were fine. And, apparently, flunking that part of the vision test on the first round is not that unusual, as evidenced by the process in place to perform a second test.

Turns out, I'd failed the regional vision exam simply because of dehydration. Thanks to my raging nerves, I hadn't drunk any water all day—not a drop from four in the morning to late afternoon. So by the end of the day, when it was finally time for me to take the highly sensitive vision test, I was dehydrated. Normally this wouldn't be a big deal. However, unbeknownst to me at the time, dehydration can affect your ability to detect microscopic depth-perception changes.

Who knew?

Fortunately, I'd wanted to pass badly enough to ask the question, "Is there another test I can take?" Many do ask that question, but others don't, and they lose their chance right out of the gate to go for the dream of flying merely because someone told them no and encouraged them down a different path. If I hadn't doggedly pursued another option—getting my eyes tested further—it would've all been over right there. The end of my dream. Thankfully, at that moment, I showed tenacity, and it made all the difference.

More tenacity would be required, though—from me and from all of my fellow naval aviator hopefuls—as we fought our way to a position in AOCS. The screening is incredibly intense, and of course I understand why. Naval aviation is renowned for the tough demands it places upon its aviators—more so than any other service. The skill, concentration, and physical performance required to land on an aircraft carrier deck, pitching on the open sea in the middle of the night with nowhere else to land, is immense. Many people possess these qualities, but few are ever challenged to use them to their full potential. So in order to even qualify for the flight-training program, we candidates would have to pass the special aviation aptitude tests and extensive psychological and physical exams at the regional level. And *then*, after losing many from among our ranks to regionals, we'd make our way to Pensacola to face the dreaded "NAMI Whammy."

"NAMI" refers to the Naval Aerospace Medical Institute, the

center of aviation medicine. This is another place where dreams go to die. It's here that we naval aviator hopefuls would try to pass the Naval Aviation Entrance Physical Evaluation. The purpose of the NAEPE is to expose you to as much naval aviation as possible in the few days you are at Pensacola. Most aviators and aviator candidates shudder at the prospect, because NAMI could give you the "Whammy" for even the slightest physical defect. If you have any sort of physical ailment or limitation—bad back, bad knees, bad eyes, bad concussions, even bad attitude—NAMI is sure to find it, and you will be done.

While in Pensacola, you also have to take a physical fitness test to show that at AOCS you will be able to withstand the countless hours devoted to physical training. In addition to a daily morning workout that usually consists of long battalion runs, untold hours are spent at AOCS performing mountain climbers, burpees, push-ups, etc. Anyone who is not in excellent physical condition upon arrival at AOCS doesn't stand a chance of making it through even the first week.

During the initial NAEPE, my group of hopefuls lost several candidates to the NAMI Whammy—people who were unable to pass either the physical fitness test or the swim screening. Navy aviators and naval flight officers must be excellent swimmers; they must be capable of surviving in the roughest, most treacherous open-ocean conditions. So all aviation officer candidates must have certain basic swimming skills to begin the program. Over the course of training, all aviation officer candidates must successfully complete extensive, exhausting, and oftentimes scary water survival training in order to graduate.

We also lost a handful of candidates who dropped out after a one-hour Q&A with the Marine Corps drill instructors.

One thing is for sure: Our numbers were dwindling quickly, and we hadn't even started yet. It was surprising and fascinating, because some of these potential candidates looked like poster-perfect aviators: square jaw, amazing physique, brilliant mind, quick wit, lots of attitude. And they didn't make it through the first day.

Nevertheless, I was among the chunk that did make it through. So, in February 1991, fresh out of the University of Wisconsin, I landed back in Pensacola, Florida—the Cradle of Aviation, as it's called—for the official beginning of AOCS. If I got through and got commissioned as a naval officer, I'd go on to flight school and continue my training there for twelve to twenty-four months. And then it would finally happen: I'd be designated a naval aviator, earn my Wings of Gold, and accept a follow-on seven-year active-duty obligation.

That is, if I could stick to it long enough.

Tenacity: The Second Element of Fearless Leadership

My depth-perception ordeal and the dreaded NAMI Whammy were just tiny forerunners of the numerous situations that would demand extreme commitment as I made my way to becoming a naval aviator and an effective leader. While the courage we discussed in the previous chapter is fundamental to leadership, it alone can't sustain you; you also have to have tenacity, the second element of fearless leadership. When you're tenacious as a leader, you're by definition unstoppable: You've found a worthy objective, and you simply won't quit until you succeed.

"Aren't courage and tenacity kind of the same thing, though?" some might ask. Well, they're similar, in that they both describe a state of mental or moral strength. But while courage is about going for it even when you feel doubt and discomfort, *tenacity* adds a new dimension: the persistence it takes to *keep* going after your goal, even when it demands a lot of you. In other words, it took courage for me to decide to go against the grain and pursue a military career that women did not previously choose, but it was tenacity that got me through the daily trials of AOCS, flight school, my work as a pilot, and my post-military career. Similarly, it takes courage for leaders of any stripe to step up, boldly declare, "Why not me?" and push themselves out of their comfort zone. But it takes tenacity to *keep* pushing and striving and working hard when the novelty of that first, decisive moment wears off, when the path ahead looks bleak or full of drudgery and challenges. Courage is the twenty-second sprint; tenacity is the five-hour marathon.

COURAGE IS THE TWENTY-SECOND SPRINT; TENACITY IS THE FIVE-HOUR MARATHON.

Without the willingness to keep at it, success in any way, shape, or form will not be possible. We all have different definitions of success, depending on our goals: graduating from college, providing clean water to children in the Third World, kicking cancer, earning a big promotion, increasing your team's sales by the end of the quarter, or even planting a garden that doesn't fail within two weeks.

On the road to any worthwhile achievement, you're going to hit those roadblocks, the moments that call for perseverance if you want to accomplish your goal. Oftentimes the greatest battle you can wage against fear and against failure occurs not on the outside, but inside your head. Fearless leaders prep themselves for that reality by building up their tenacity muscle until it's strong enough to take them as far as they want to go—to bust through those barriers.

So, how can you stoke your inner tenacity so you have the commitment, drive, and persistence it takes to lead?

Get Ready to Work—Hard

Not everyone in life gets to run a business or lead a team, but in my years in the Navy and my years as a leadership consultant, I've noticed one trait that consistently separates those who just dream big from those who go out there and *do* big: the ability and drive to work hard.

After working with numerous Fortune 100 and Fortune 500 clients in programs where I help individual contributors, aspiring managers, salespeople, and executives further develop their leadership skills, I can tell you from firsthand experience that those participants who are committed to doing the work required to lead fare much better than those participants who just sit back and expect the magic to happen. That's just the way things work. If you want to become a stronger leader, you must be willing to step up, show up, and put in the time!

The story of S. Truett Cathy—the founder, chairman, and CEO of Chick-fil-A—is a great example. Cathy once said that "the difference between success and failure is often about five percent more effort," and his personal history shows that he really believes it.

The sixth of seven children, Cathy was born in 1921 to a very poor family. By the time he was eight years old, he was selling refreshments in his front yard. By age twelve, he had a paper route. Upon graduation from high school, he enlisted in the Army, and after leaving the military, he built a small restaurant with his brother—it included ten stools, four tables, and some chairs.

Cathy and his brother worked long, hard hours trying to make the restaurant a success. Then tragedy struck: Cathy's brother died in a plane crash with another brother and two of their friends. S. Truett Cathy was left to carry on alone. In 1951, he opened a second restaurant, determined to make it succeed. "With two restaurants, if I wasn't having problems in one, I was having problems in the other," he said later. And yet he pushed on, refusing to give up and remaining committed to working a little bit harder than the next guy.

Nearly twenty years later—*twenty years!*—Cathy opened the first Chick-fil-A restaurant, featuring his chicken sandwich that had been popular with his early customers. The rest is history. Today, more than 45,000 people are employed by Chick-fil-A restaurants, and the brand has expanded rapidly.

How badly do you want to lead well? Are you willing to persist for twenty years, if that's what it takes? Think about it. If you want the glory of leadership without any of the grunt work, forget it! Won't happen. Just talking about becoming a leader and saying that you want to become a leader is not the same as doing the hard work to become a better leader. You can want to become a leader really, really badly, but if you're not willing to work for it—if you don't have focus and tenacity—you won't get there. You can't be all blow, no go.

Some people tend to think, *Well, I want this really bad, so I should get it!* Or we just gab about what we want to do and hope our bright new future materializes. But that's not how it works. Odds are, you're not taking action because your fearful side is soothing you into thinking that you can put off being a leader. If you want to be fearless, though, you're going to have to put in a lot of time doing difficult—and frankly, sometimes boring—work. There's no shortcut around this, and a lot of potential leaders falter before they get a chance to lead, because they're just not ready to do the grunt work.

If I had a penny for every time I've heard someone start a sentence with, "I really wanted to do this, but . . . ," I'd have a *lot* of pennies. It's the "but" that gets in the way of success, and all too often what lies on the other side of this obstacle is a heap of hard work. The most successful people in the world do the things they know they need to be doing even when they don't feel like doing them. It's simple, but it's not easy.

Climbing Till Your Heart Explodes

On the first day of AOCS, tensions were high, the fear in the air was palpable, and before day's end, many who had thought they were committed to this intense training program were already on their way home.

> # THE MOST SUCCESSFUL PEOPLE IN THE WORLD DO THE THINGS THEY KNOW THEY NEED TO BE DOING EVEN WHEN THEY DON'T FEEL LIKE DOING THEM.

AOCS consisted of four basic phases—academic, military, physical fitness, and swimming, each with its own challenges. We learned about naval organization, operations, and law; United States sea power; seamanship; naval leadership; engineering; aerodynamics; air navigation; aviation physiology; survival (land and sea); and much more. And on top of all that came a metric shit-ton of physical training. This wasn't easy stuff, and we were told over and over of the spectacular attrition rate: around 50 percent of us wouldn't make it through AOCS.

On the day I first met my drill instructor, Gunnery Sergeant Woodring, I realized just how much work officer training was going to require. That first morning, at zero dark thirty, I was awakened by several lovely young gentlemen screaming in my ear. Within minutes, I was out of bed and surrounded by five drill instructors, one of them my brother's former USMC drill instructor just a year prior—and all of them screaming at the top of their lungs as clothes, mattresses, pillows, sheets, and blankets flew everywhere. It was pure chaos.

I can still remember the first words Gunnery Sergeant Woodring ever shouted at me: "Get downstairs in the grass and mountain-climb 'til your heart explodes!"

I guess that was his way of saying, "Welcome aboard."

I got to know quite a few of these drill instructors in an up-close-and-personal manner—including an intimate view of throbbing veins and a constant stream of colorful and innovative commentary that I truly have not heard since. Their ability to make words up while screaming at you or running in formation was legendary. And it was definitely not for your grandmother's ear. I'm a tall gal, and I'll never forget the frustration of one of the shorter drill instructors whose Smokey-the-Bear brim came about to my boobs. The occasional love tap of that hat brim on my chest was usually followed by creative punishments and earned me even more colorful commentary than usual in front of the other candidates.

At the time, each class of sixty-five to eighty officer candidates usually included five or six women. I learned early on during AOCS that not a single female who had ever started with my particular drill instructor actually finished the class with him. Not one! My odds were not looking good. And this was to be his last class of officer candidates before retiring from the United States Marine Corps. I focused on learning all I could from this highly practiced professional. I was fiercely determined to graduate under his tutelage—and break his record.

In some kinder, gentler circles, what we went through *might* be considered hazing, but we didn't consider it that. We knew we had to earn the right to be there. This was separating the wheat from the chaff, the strong from the weak. Our drill instructors were finding out who could hack it and who couldn't. They were finding our pressure points and attempting to exert as much force on them as possible. They were identifying the people who weren't prepared to handle the stress, who couldn't work through the challenges—both physical and mental—we would face. They had to uncover who had the tenacity to keep after their objective, no matter what—and who did not.

Those who didn't have the tenacity required would quit the program, or "drop on request" (DOR). All naval aviation-training courses are voluntary. At any time in training, up until an officer candidate or student naval aviator becomes a winged aviator, that person has the option to request termination of training. All it takes is a word or two from the candidate. Anytime an officer candidate makes a statement such as "I quit" or "DOR," he or she is instantly removed from that training environment and the out-processing procedures are started immediately. In my experience, at no time was an officer candidate ever encouraged to stay in the program once those words were uttered—removal was lightning fast.

The same is true of leadership: You don't *have* to do anything. At any moment, you can back away, go with the flow, and regress back to your comfort zone. But that's not what fearless leaders do. They dig in, dig deep, and keep working.

> **FEARLESS LEADERS DIG IN, DIG DEEP, AND KEEP WORKING.**

I learned so many lessons in AOCS. These were the old days, and more often than not the bits of wisdom and important lessons were dispensed while we were facedown in a puddle of sweat doing knuckle push-ups, or doing jumping jacks (or "side-straddle hops," as they were affectionately referred to) until it felt as though our calves would burst or our Achilles tendons would snap. "Climb 'til your heart explodes!" Woodring had screamed at me. Some days it really felt as if that would happen.

Yet not all the tests of our tenacity required long hours studying or sweating away at push-ups and burpees. One particularly memorable trial involved nothing but me and a pen.

"So you want to fly?" Gunnery Sergeant Woodring asked. "Okay. Go stand with your back against the wall while holding out this government-issue black pen. Let's see how bad you really want to fly!"

Try holding a pen straight out from your body, keeping it parallel to the deck floor—for an hour or two. You'll be surprised how heavy a teeny little pen can get. You'll discover muscles in places you didn't even know existed, and they might want to give up—but you won't let them. That takes tenacity.

With a bucketful of tenacity and grit, I eventually made it through AOCS; 50 percent of my classmates did not. Graduation and earning that first salute from now newly promoted Master Sergeant Woodring was one of the proudest days of my life. Because, you see, once we made it through Aviation Officer Candidate School, that salute was my very first one as an officer. Now Master Sergeant Woodring would be taking orders from me (although only until his retirement).

Next stop: flight school.

How Bad Do You Want It?

The first morning of orientation at Naval Air Station Corpus Christi, Texas, occurred in a typical hangar briefing space: tidy, a few aircraft pictures hanging on the walls, miniature models of T-34s dangling from the chalkboard's eraser ledge, to be used for instruction and maneuver demonstrations. As we waited for the "welcome aboard" briefing from an instructor pilot, there was a lot of nervous laughter, sweaty palms, fidgeting, and joking around. There were plenty of sideways glances as fellow student naval aviators sized up the competition. Who would make it through? Who would fail? Who would be the best?

Our welcome aboard came from an experienced Marine Corps aviator instructor pilot. The briefing began with all the niceties: "Welcome aboard, this is going to be exciting, yada, yada, yada." And then it took a turn. Sitting at every desk was an identical stack of books a foot and a half tall. We were told that we would be responsible for knowing everything contained in those books, soup to nuts, in the next six weeks. Otherwise we would "wash out"—that is, we wouldn't make it through the program. So if we weren't able to drink from the fire hose, this occupation was not for us.

Then we were told to look at our neighbor to the left and to the right. Over the course of the next couple of years, at least one of the three of us—a third of the class at a *minimum*—would no longer be with us. This class would inevitably shrink, either by attrition (flunking out) or by death.

Very few times in the history of the world has a room gone so quiet, so quickly. This was not a game.

We were all visibly shocked. A few guys left right then and there! It was a bit of a traumatic experience for some would-be student aviators. They had beat the 50 percent attrition rate of AOCS, or graduated from the Naval Academy, or gone through ROTC. But this? This realization put them over the edge. The reality of the workload and the risk involved hit too close to home for some.

We all had to ask ourselves: Did we have the courage and tenacity to do the work and grind this out?

I tried to put things in perspective. There was a syllabus (not risky, right?), and as long as you pretty much duct-taped yourself to the couch, chair, etc., and *put in the work*, you would eventually get through all that reading and memorizing. It was no small task, and definitely not for those who kinda sorta wanted to be an aviator, but it could be done. Among my colleagues, different people had different tricks for memorizing all the information—no different from people who are going through medical school.

But then you had to put all that knowledge into action. You had to actually think *and* fly—at the same time. You may scoff at that, thinking it's not that much different from thinking and driving, which isn't so difficult (though even in a car you can cause a lot of damage by daydreaming). But ask any military aviation instructor, and he or she will tell you that more than one super-smart aerospace engineer has been unable to think, fly, and talk on the radios, all at the same time.

In flight school, a solid work ethic could be the difference between making it through this program successfully and going home with your hat in your helmet bag. Your grit was put to the test. All these obstacles challenged your commitment to what you said you wanted and revealed whether you were actually committed to working for it.

Growing up in Green Bay, Wisconsin—a place where people tend to have a tremendous work ethic—gave me a huge advantage going into flight school. Not only that, but I had spent four years at the University of Wisconsin as a varsity rower—a Division I athlete with some time at the pre-Olympic level.

Rowing is a brutal sport, one that predates nearly all the modern Olympic games. It brings with it none of the modern-day trappings of other high-level sports: fame, money, glory, and lucrative contracts. Those who are attracted to rowing are not driven by these things; they are simply *driven*—not only to compete, but to test their own limits.

You endure months and months of training in isolation. You refuse to let your teammates down, so you push, using every ounce of energy to go farther and harder. You ignore the burning in your lungs, the flames in your quads and calves, and the voice in your brain, screaming at you to stop.

You row. You do the work. Welcome to the Pain Train.

In order to become a fearless leader, you can't be afraid to do the work, to know that there will be highs and lows and that sometimes you will want to quit. But that's what leadership is about: sticking it out.

Do you remember a pre–Angry Birds world? I do. But those little birdies almost didn't make it home to roost. Finnish developer Rovio had gone through eight years and fifty-one failed games, trying to create a hit. For Rovio, the fifty-second time was the charm. The company leaders' willingness to stick with it and persevere, even in the face of failure after failure, is the stuff gaming legends are made of. With each and every failure, they learned a little more and became more determined to try again.

Almost everyone has heard the quote from Thomas Edison, when asked about his more than 10,000 failed attempts at making a working light bulb: "I have not failed. I've just found 10,000 ways that won't work."

Fearless leaders work hard. How many times have you heard "Work smarter, not harder?" Well, I think that's BS. You have to work smart *and* hard.

Ouch.

Colin Powell, a former four-star general and the first African-American appointed as the US secretary of state, famously said, "There are no secrets to success. It is the result of preparation, hard work, and learning from failure."

You say you're a dreamer? Well, here's a thought on that from makeup mogul Estée Lauder: "I never dreamed about success. I worked for it."

Looking for thoughts from someone more *au courant*? Gary Vaynerchuk, known as Gary V. to his devoted tribe, is a wildly successful serial entrepreneur. His perspective? "We're living through a period right now where we have a lot of very smart people looking at math, and analytics, and efficiencies," says Vaynerchuk. "I think those are all great things to take pride in, but I also think you need to put in the work . . . You can call out all the best business opportunities you want, but the bottom line is that nobody ever got paid to make snow angels."[10]

You can't work hard just some of the time, either. High-performing individuals, those people who are truly interested in peak performance, are always willing to go a little farther, do a little bit more. If you're willing to work hard only sometimes, it won't make a big difference. Developing a solid work ethic is tough, but it's what separates the ultra-successful from the average. If you're looking to separate yourself from your peers, you need to be willing to outwork them. Period.

IF YOU'RE LOOKING TO SEPARATE YOURSELF FROM YOUR PEERS, YOU NEED TO BE WILLING TO OUTWORK THEM. PERIOD.

Embracing the Suck

Here's a little strategy for getting through the hard work that's going to be required: In the Navy, we say you should "embrace the suck." What does that mean? Just what it sounds like: Recognize that this work is part of getting to your goal, that it sucks, and that you're going to give it a big hug and do it anyway.

Be willing to do what others are not—and try to enjoy it as much as you can, however perversely. Be willing to work harder than everyone else around you. As they say, luck is simply the meeting of preparation (i.e., hard work) and opportunity. If you're not willing to put the work in, you're like the students in flight school who took one look at the stack of books and walked out.

I can look back at my time in AOCS as one where discipline and commitment were drilled into those of us who dared to stay, who dared to be pushed past our limits. Those who stayed were committed, highly motivated, and truly dedicated; we were willing to work through the crap. That fearless attitude, that tenacity—or its absence—determined our success or our failure. Every challenge could be framed as an opportunity and every failure as a lesson learned. It was a great platform not only for the rigors of aviation, but for life as well. Sometimes we had to embrace the suck, and we knew it.

In the world of leadership, even with a fantastic job, things aren't going to be fun all the time. But if you want to succeed as a leader, you embrace the suck—you grind it out and do the work anyway.

Develop a Bias for Action

I once heard an executive at a company sales kickoff meeting say that the key to success is to "dream big." This guy delivered his message with charisma, but I respectfully disagree. Dreaming big is great, but the real key to achieving any goal in life is to *do* big. That holds especially true for leaders. There's no better way to build the tenacity you need to lead than by building a predisposition for *doing*—a bias for action.

To become more tenacious as a leader, you have to go out and do it—and the "doing it" comes first. When you learn to take action even in situations where you feel stuck, frustrated, or intimidated, you increase your ability to get through situations that demand commitment.

It's in the moments of hesitation and inaction that we're most prone to giving up. But when you train yourself to take the initiative in demanding or frustrating situations—when you teach yourself to just *do* it—you've added an essential weapon in the fearless leader's arsenal.

The difference between who you are and who you want to be is *what you do.* And you may not like what you have to do in order to get where you want to be. It may not be pretty, and it may not come easily. To be successful, however, you must be willing to take action when and where others do not. Act decisively, and take the initiative.

THE DIFFERENCE BETWEEN WHO YOU ARE AND WHO YOU WANT TO BE IS *WHAT YOU DO*.

In AOCS, everything was done to weed out people who, when scared and under stress, didn't take the initiative and couldn't execute. Those people didn't understand how to develop a bias for action.

Why did all this matter? Well, when you're trying to come aboard a pitching ship in a strike fighter aircraft at 165 miles per hour, or you're getting launched by a catapult, going from zero to more than 180 miles per hour in less than two seconds, and the Air Boss screams through the radio, "Tomcat off the bow! Eject! Eject! Eject!" there is no gray area. You don't ask questions or take time to think it over; you have to take action, or you will die.

That's why our instructors worked hard to establish a bias for action, passing only those student aviators who demonstrated that they would be instantly ready take on any challenge. It is drilled into all of our aspiring aviation officer candidates: Be flexible. Act decisively. Take the initiative. Don't wait to be told what to do. Your life and the lives of others depend on this.

This bias for action is as critical to survival in business as it is in aviation. Fearless leaders can't wait to see how things go. They can't hold back! They have to move forward. They have to act.

Karl E. Weick, a respected organizational theorist, tells a story in his book *Sensemaking in Organizations* about of a group of soldiers lost in a storm in the Alps during World War II.[11] The group has just about given up hope of ever getting out of the mountains alive, when someone miraculously finds a map among the gear. Following this map, they manage to get back to the base and safety. Only after making their narrow escape from death by freezing did they discover that the map was not of the Alps but of the Pyrenees. The map had given the soldiers motivation to *act,* and it was that action itself rather than the map that got them out alive.

Research shows, too, that action reduces fear—it helps us become fearless. Seymour Epstein of the University of Massachusetts at Amherst conducted a study in which novice parachute jumpers were fitted with heart rate monitors that measured their pulse as the plane climbed upward toward its release point. He found that the jumpers' heart rates got faster and faster until just before they jumped. But once they were out of the plane, their heart rates declined dramatically.[12] The most stressful part of the entire experience was the anticipation; the stress was, in effect, an illusion. Once the reality of the event (free-falling) took over, the fear vanished.

There is a Zen saying: "Leap, and the net will appear." It's true! Those moments right before you *do* something are the worst. Rip off the Band-Aid. Jump. You'll grow your wings on the way down. And the next time you are scared to take that next step, to take a chance, to make a dreaded phone call, to tell someone no, you'll take the initiative a little bit sooner. You'll start doing the work instead of sitting in the bleachers waiting—suffocated by dread, paralyzed by fear—and wondering, *What if . . .?*

Find a Third Way

While flying the A-4 Skyhawk in the advanced strike fighter pipeline, I had only about two and a half months of advanced training left before earning my naval aviator Wings of Gold when I hit another bump in the road.

OK, more like a brick wall.

As part of our training evolution, we all went out to El Centro, California, for a huge weapons training detachment. We were to be evaluated and graded on our individual abilities: dropping bombs on targets with accuracy, performing a lot of dynamic, low-level flights, shooting rockets, and strafing ground targets. All the fun stuff.

But in the middle of one of our pre-detachment weapons briefings, surrounded by roughly forty-five other student naval aviators, I was pulled out of the briefing and sent to the commanding officer's office—which is *never* a good thing.

The CO had the head of the Navy's Detailing Division, responsible for giving out follow-on assignments, on speakerphone—another bad sign. The detailer proceeded to tell me that since the combat exclusion clause had not been lifted yet, and the Navy was getting rid of the other aircraft that women had flown in the past, I had two choices: I could either get out of the Navy completely, with no additional time obligation, or I could change designators—go to a non-flying job—with *no chance* of ever flying again.

When I had started flight school, the Department of Defense was still squabbling over lifting the combat exclusion clause, which prohibited women from flying combat aircraft. These combat aircraft strike fighters are regarded as the ultimate assignment, so at the end of your advanced jet flight training, which can take up to two years, only those with the top grades are assigned to strike fighters. Combat jets—that's what I wanted, and now I couldn't achieve it.

I. Was. Crushed.

I was sent back into the weapons briefing with my fellow students—all men—and looked around the room. Everything I had worked so hard for was gone, simply because I was female, while every other male aviator got to continue on—just because they were men. Not because they were more qualified; because they were men.

I wasn't okay with that.

I waited until the briefing was done, collected my thoughts, and headed back to the commanding officer's office. Even without knowing what the future held for me, I made a decision. I suggested to the CO that there was no way I was going to quit, but I didn't want to stop flying either, so we needed to figure out another option. A third way.

It was a risk, and I made a judgment call without a lot of information. But what if I had waited for more information? Who knows where I would have ended up? In Keflavik, Iceland, maybe, manning a wind turbine. No offense to Keflavik or the wind turbine industry, but that's not what I wanted. I had to take the initiative. Sometimes failure to take action is the biggest failure of all.

And here is where performance matters. Because I had done so well and performed so consistently, my CO went to bat for me. He went up the chain of command to his boss, and then his boss went to *his* boss, and in the end they decided to cut orders that allowed me, after receiving my wings, to stay on as a flight instructor for eighteen months. I'd be training men to fly. But my CO and his superiors were also buying me time in hopes that the combat exclusion clause would be lifted and I would be able to move on professionally with the rest of my peers to a combat squadron.

When the rules changed, I was prepared. The combat exclusion clause was lifted in April 1993. By then I was at the top of my class, fully qualified and positioned to go fly fighters.

Finding a third way isn't about being stubborn; it's about looking for other ways to get done what needs to be done. It's about showing tenacity even when you feel like giving up. The system said there was no place for me—and I said, "I'm not going to accept that."

Don't give up when there is still the possibility that you can be successful! Go out and push on the system. Don't take no as your first answer. It's about being proactive, exercising initiative—being willing to win in a different way. Adapt and figure it out.

Keep Your Goal Out Front

Hard work, in and of itself, might be good for the soul. But if we want our hard work to pay off, we have to know why we're doing it. When you have that reason right in front of you, you're ten times more likely than the next person to persist when times get a little rough: when you encounter a scary situation, when someone tells you no, or when the job before you is going to take a whole bucketful of elbow grease.

Writing down or keeping a visual reminder of your goals, your *why*, is a terrific way to give you a tenacity boost when the going gets rough. If you've painted a vibrant picture of what success looks like, you can turn to that picture for encouragement when you feel like giving up.

IF WE WANT OUR HARD WORK TO PAY OFF, WE HAVE TO KNOW WHY WE'RE DOING IT.

What's the "one thing" for you? What is that singular goal that you want to reach? You need to be crystal clear on that if you ever want to get there. During uncertain or tumultuous times, instead of just hoping you can hang on to your job, focus and think about where you want to be in three years—or five. Then map a course of action and take steps *every day* toward achieving that goal, that dream. Need more training? Go get it. Need a mentor? Find one. Need a bigger network of friends and associates? Pick up the damned phone! Your mental image of that goal will drive you to carry out the action you must take.

At AOCS, our vision of success was graduating and moving on in pursuit of those Wings of Gold. I knew that I wanted to fly a combat fighter aircraft—period. That vision helped me hang on to my dream as I sought out a third way, after being told that I wouldn't have the professional opportunity I so desperately wanted just because I was a woman. I knew what I wanted for my future picture, and that allowed me to make the right choices to get there, to earn the naval aviator's Wings of Gold. I kept my goal out front, concentrating with fierce resolve and determination on becoming a combat pilot—and I didn't give up. I stayed focused on what mattered.

Those of us who had made it almost to the end of flight school still had some of the toughest flying yet to do—the air combat and aircraft carrier qualification phases. To help us through, we relied on a visual reminder that was right in front of us every time we would walk into the ready room, where the squadron duty officer would run the flight schedule of the day and where all the student naval aviators and instructor pilots would gather before briefings, after flights, after debriefs . . . In fact, the ready room was generally just a fantastic place to tell stories and hang out.

Near the entrance to the ready room was a shadow box—a frame with a clear piece of glass over it. It contained a group of patches with student naval aviators' names and gold aviator wings embroidered on a flight-suit patch. Every day, my fellow students and I filed past this reminder of our goal, knowing that as we got closer to meeting our goal, our names, too, would be on a patch in that shadow box. It served as an important visual reminder of what would come next if we could just hang in there.

A vision of success boosts your ability to stubbornly fight on—even when the system tries to get in the way of your goal, even when it feels as if that pen you're holding parallel to the deck weighs five tons. We *need* that vision today more than ever, precisely because our ADD-afflicted culture can easily knock us off our game. With abundant opportunities and a constant bombardment of messages, we frequently lose sight of why we're doing something, especially when it's something that seems so hard. *Why not do this other thing instead? Or how about this option? What you're trying now, it's just not worth all this work!* Your vision of the future helps silence those pesky voices. It will help you to remember that pain is temporary, and to delay gratification in service of your big goal.

You see, goals are not random rainbows high in the clouds; they are practical objectives that are intended to produce concrete results.

You can achieve just about anything if you want it badly enough and are willing to pursue it with single-minded determination. The choice is yours.

Go for It, One Bite at a Time

We all know the old joke about how to eat an elephant ("one bite at a time!"). It may be a chestnut, but it holds a reliable seed of truth. It's so very easy to get overwhelmed by your big goal and all that it's going to take to get there, but if you start by chunking down that goal into bite-sized pieces rather than trying to swallow the whole beast at once, you'll supercharge your tenacity and lower your risk of getting discouraged.

During AOCS, in the middle of its legendary behavior modification training, or in PT (physical training), by the thousandth jumping jack, sometimes it felt as though my calves were about to explode. People would say things like, "I can't do this for three more months!" The winners, despite definitely feeling that way as well, would take a different perspective: "I can make it to lunch time," or "I can get through the next five minutes," or "I can do fifty more." That perspective gives you fuel to keep on pushing just to the top of the next hill. It gives you something to focus on in the present rather than an overwhelming goal too far in the future.

Keep in mind that by taking it one step at a time, you haven't lost sight of the goal; you've just committed to making it through the next five minutes, the next set of mountain climbers, the next aerodynamics test. Because those little bites of the elephant lead to your true goal.

Of course, chopping up big goals into small steps doesn't make your path to leadership *easy*; it still requires a lot of work to keep on going. Some days in AOCS, success was just making it through ten more burpees, running one more mile, getting through a swim test as a team, or not falling asleep in class—and that was difficult enough. But remember that if you decide to quit, you'll never know if success lay just on the other side of that one small step you gave up on!

Clearly, it takes time to build that tenacity muscle; it doesn't just magically appear because you wish for it. The best thing to do, then, is to start taking small steps today.

We sometimes look at leaders who've done great things and think, *Man, I could never do that.* We forget that most of these people didn't have a meteoric rise. Their success is the result of tiny bursts of courage and tenacity—millions of them!—over the course of years or decades. Oscar-winning actor Adrien Brody said, "My dad told me, 'It takes fifteen years to be an overnight success,' and it took me seventeen-and-a-half years." In other words, it took one small bite of the elephant after another, each taking him farther from his comfort zone and closer to his goals.

The beauty of the one-bite-at-a-time approach is that it's pretty much Psychology 101. Nearly every human is hardwired to desire improvement—to make progress. We all want to get better at the things we do. When you break an otherwise difficult task into more manageable steps, you start to see progress, and that feeds your innate desire for mastery. Once you've stimulated that drive, you're going to have positive reinforcement as you press through the challenges that every leader faces. And you'll be prepared to take on new challenges as well.

Leaders and managers face staggeringly complex challenges on a regular basis, which is what makes this skill for chunking the impossible into "small wins" so valuable to them. In business today, when you consider the time, energy, and money expended on all the continuous improvement programs and operational excellence processes thrown at organizations, too many companies still fail at the basics.

I was brought in to work with a leading global manufacturing company that had numerous wildly successful plants—and several spectacularly underperforming ones that were dragging the company's bottom line down. This organization was in dire straits.

In the opening conversations, I learned that the managers on both sides of the fence—the superstar side and the underperforming side—wanted no part of the process. It was too overwhelming. Each group thought it was the other guys' problem. The prevailing attitude was "We can't fix this . . . It's just too much . . . It's not my fault." I actually overheard all these comments.

Many hours, heated debates, smoke breaks, Post-it notes, and flip charts later, we uncovered the fact that some very straightforward things were not being done. There was no sharing of best practices or lessons learned. These are table stakes for a fighter pilot. Sharing of best practices saves our lives. Best of all, some simple fixes were all that was required to get the underperformers headed in the right direction.

What does a fearless leader do in this situation? Well, after stepping up to the plate and displaying the courage to take on the venture in the first place, you ask good questions and then start chunking up the tasks that need immediate action. If you want to get the place functioning again, start with something small and manageable.

So we asked the plant managers some probing questions about the problems they were facing, their missed opportunities, and what currently worked and what didn't. Using that feedback, we assembled managers within the plants and put together not just a vision of where the plant would go, but also a plan for what they would start doing *the next day.* We wanted these leaders to get some small wins under their belts, to gain traction—to get back on that path to excellence.

* * *

Fearless leaders have to keep being tenacious, even when they feel they've reached success. As a leader, you have to keep on taking the first step, initiating changes, projects, or communication that is necessary for the organization. Nothing says "leader" like being the initiator.

Once you've completed an accomplishment or even reached what feels like the pinnacle of success, don't expect it to be easy to stay there. It's human nature to revel in success, to pat yourself on the back and think, *Ahhhh, I've finally made it!* But if you want to move on to an even higher place—or even just keep your spot—you have to stay tenacious.

The second you start feeling as though you've made it, and allow yourself to be less fearless, less courageous, less tenacious—that's precisely when the ninja called complacency sneaks up and throat-chops you. Next up? Failure.

Even though I am all for celebrating successes, it's essential to keep your eye on the future and keep persevering. It's too easy to become satisfied with your current performance and fail to keep striving to increase your performance level.

Tenacious leaders can achieve great results. Remarkable success does not require genius or great education. It does not require luck, a rare genetic gift, or superhero powers. It does, however, require the ability to choose a goal, create a plan, work hard, and stay the course.

At the end of the day, tenacity does even more than get you where you want to go. When a leader consistently displays tenacity, the people he or she is leading notice—and begin to follow that lead. In that way, tenacious leaders give the gift of tenacity to their team, supercharging the team's effectiveness as a whole.

TENACIOUS LEADERS GIVE THE GIFT OF TENACITY TO THEIR TEAM, SUPERCHARGING THE TEAM'S EFFECTIVENESS AS A WHOLE.

The same is true with all three of the fundamental traits of fearless leaders. When you're courageous, your people will become more courageous. When you're tenacious, your people will become more tenacious. And perhaps most important of all is modeling the third fundamental trait—integrity—for your team. Read on to learn exactly how and why you should make integrity a cornerstone of your leadership approach.

Chapter 3

INTEGRITY

EARNING TRUST BY DOING WHAT'S RIGHT

*Integrity is one of those words that many people keep in that
desk drawer labeled "too hard." It's not a topic for the dinner
table or the cocktail party. You can't buy or sell it. When
supported with education, a person's integrity can give him
something to rely on when his perspective seems to blur, when
rules and principles seem to waver, and when he's faced with
hard choices of right or wrong.*
—*Vice Admiral James Bond Stockdale, USN*

One of the legendary heroes of the Vietnam War is Vice Admiral James
Stockdale. After his A-4 Skyhawk was shot down just south of Hanoi
in North Vietnam, as one of the senior ranking officers in the prison
camp known as the Hanoi Hilton, he endured and survived seven and
a half years of torture, interrogation, and solitary confinement at the
hands of the Communist Vietnamese.

Admiral Stockdale often relayed the story that occasionally, while in prison, he would get a message via tap code from a new fellow prisoner of war. The tap code was the system that the POWs used to communicate with one another. They would tap on the walls with their knuckles, employing a code that consisted of a 5 x 5 matrix of the alphabet, where each letter was identified by its location on the matrix. (For an alphabet of twenty-five letters, the *C* was used to replace any *K*s.) The first number identified the letter's row location and the second number identified the letter's column location. So an *S* would be four taps followed by three taps (or three taps followed by four taps). The question new POWs often asked Admiral Stockdale was about how to survive. "I've got to have something to hang on to," they would plead. "What do you think I should hold as my highest value in here?" He answered with what he believed to his core: "The guy next door. Protect him. Love him. He is precious. He is your only link with our prisoner civilization in here."[13]

On more than one occasion, Admiral Stockdale and other POWs were willing to live with integrity, to stand up for the men to their left and to their right, even knowing that it would most likely lead to further beatings, pain, and quite possibly death. Even though he was far from home and in a hostile environment, and even though his choices and behaviors would likely never come to light, Admiral Stockdale didn't abandon his moral responsibility to make decisions with integrity—even when risking the ultimate sacrifice.

More than once, Admiral Stockdale refused to answer questions about his fellow POWs or was caught secretly communicating with them, knowing full well he would be beaten to within an inch of his life as a consequence. In his many years of captivity, he suffered multiple broken bones, was contorted by inhumane "rope tricks" that would leave his arms useless for weeks, and endured month after month of solitary confinement in leg irons—all because he wouldn't give up basic information about his fellow soldiers. Several months into his captivity, he discovered that there were actually captured men senior to him who completely vacated their leadership positions, refusing to communicate with, engage with, or provide any support—any *hope*—to their broken, desperate, and sobbing soldiers. This clearly was a lapse in integrity. Right and wrong was up for grabs, and these other so-called leaders chose the easy path. And prisoners died because of this abandonment and lack of leadership.

Part of leading with integrity is constantly putting the mission before the self. When you remain committed to the mission, when you lead by example—as did Admiral Stockdale through his behavior, even at extreme personal risk—that is true fearless leadership.

Admiral Stockdale once wrote:

> I never will forget coming home from eight years in prison [as a Vietnam War POW] and being told that the Navy would be coming out with some real tough policies about moral integrity. I was delighted and thought we were actually going to have service-wide dialogue about pilots who chicken out over the target and prisoners of war who cop out and accept parole. And then I saw the policy paper: nothing but a bunch of crap about fiscal accountability. Is that as deep into personal integrity as the system can afford to get?[14]

Integrity: The Third Element of Fearless Leadership

Courage gives you what it takes to step up and assume the mantle of leadership, and tenacity keeps you going when your role requires everything you've got. But neither of those will take you all the way to being a truly fearless leader. If you want to have any hope of inspiring the people under you to innovate and take risks—if you want to win their confidence and loyalty and work with them to do great things—you've got to have the third fundamental trait of fearless leadership: integrity.

This should be a short chapter, really: Do the right thing. Be honest. Be trustworthy. The end. Those three ideas aren't innovative or new. And yet this supposedly commonsense stuff is far from common. Having the resolve, the wisdom, and the audacity to do the right thing under difficult circumstances is not easy.

Name any great military or business leader you can think of— Admiral Stockdale, General Colin Powell, John Chambers of Cisco, General Norman Schwarzkopf, Gandhi, Jeff Bezos of Amazon, Margaret ("Meg") Whitman of eBay, Dan Cathy of Chick-fil-A, Robert Tillman of Lowe's—and think about whether that person had or has integrity. Does the person seem fully comfortable with his or her identity and willing to be true to core values? Do these people walk their talk? Are they good role models? Do they do their best to do what's right, and do they admit when they've stumbled? Are they willing to buck public opinion even when their position will be extremely unpopular? Do they "put their troops first"?

These are essential characteristics in the concept of integrity. Great leaders do these things.

Many "leaders" have grand titles, look the part, say the right things, and do just fine when the waters are calm. But sprinkle volatility into the situation, throw in some ambiguity, and add the demand for change, and all bets are off. Business models can be challenged or destroyed, and the chaotic, fast-changing environment pushes leaders at all levels to their limits. When it hits the fan, there will be those who lose their nerve, are overwhelmed with fear, and go to great depths to protect their career. Expect it. But don't get sucked into it.

Integrity means having the wisdom to understand what is right and what is wrong, and then the courage to stand firm in your principles and speak the truth, even in times of crisis or at great personal risk—consistently. This is what earns a leader trust and loyalty. The most valuable asset any leader can have is a loyal crew—and that's as true in your organization as it is in the US Navy. Fearless leaders do not *demand* loyalty, however; they know it must be earned. And the way to earn it is through upright and uncompromising character—through the consistent demonstration of integrity, in good times and bad.

> **FEARLESS LEADERS DO NOT *DEMAND* LOYALTY; THEY KNOW IT MUST BE EARNED.**

Integrity is one of the primary attributes and cornerstones of military professionalism; its importance in the armed forces really cannot be overstated. Every officer and enlisted member has this drilled into him or her from day one. And our society certainly expects integrity from its leaders, both military and professional. But regretfully, a closer look reveals an unsettling lack of integrity—even in the military, where it's so highly prized.

Integrity on the Decline

General H. Norman Schwarzkopf highlighted the importance of character when he said, "Leadership is a potent combination of strategy and character. But if you must be without one, be without strategy." Yet several studies over the past few decades suggest that lack of character and integrity among leaders is a significant problem. A US Army War College report from 1970 titled "Study on Military Professionalism" looked at integrity among Army officers.[15] Responses from all ranks of officer revealed "widespread and often significant differences between the ideal ethical/moral/professional standards of the Army—as epito-mized by 'Duty-Honor-Country'—and the prevailing standards."

A 1981 survey of US Air Force officers supports the results in the Army War College survey, showing that 63.4 percent of the students at Squadron Officer School, 89.6 percent at Air Command and Staff College, and 69.8 percent at Air War College had felt pressure from their organizations or senior officers to compromise their integrity.[16]

These results are similar to those of a survey conducted by Majors Joseph R. Daskevich and Paul A. Nafziger at the Air Command and Staff College in 1980, which found that 88 percent of the officers felt pressured, whether by their organizations or by their superiors, to compromise their integrity. All the officers—100 percent of them—felt that other officers had violated their integrity.[17]

These discussions carry on today, whether they surround sexual harassment issues, a dire lack of funding for combat troops and avi-ators, command climate problems, falsification of documents, mis-handling of classified documents—and the list goes on. Often, when these issues come to a head, leaders—commanding officers—are fired. And the majority of the reasons boil down to an essential failure in one area: integrity.

Integrity is apparently lacking in the corporate sphere, too. A survey by the American Management Association in 2002 discovered that 76 percent of managers listed ethics and integrity among their company's corporate values, yet 32 percent admitted that their compa-nies' actual practices did not match their public statements.[18] Perhaps these business leaders believe it won't serve their best interests. As Dr. Joanne Ciulla, professor and chair of Leadership and Ethics at the University of Richmond, mentions in her book *Ethics: The Heart of Leadership,* a survey of 671 executives shows that 25 percent of them believed ethics could impede a successful career.[19]

The Navy had its Tailhook debacle to contend with. The Air Force had a handful of officers implicated in a narcotics investigation at the same time as and on the same base where thirty-four nuclear launch officers were implicated in a 2014 cheating scandal. These officers were all caught cheating in an attempt to earn a 100 percent grade on an exam required to sustain their nuclear certifications.

Clearly this is all cause for worry. When one of your shared core values is integrity, such a clear and massive violation of it causes great concern. No amount of leader visits, pep talks, remedial training, or greater oversight will fix this. Such external controls have nothing to do with integrity.

Whether you are an officer manning a missile silo and taking shortcuts, a Navy aircraft squadron skipper who feels a need to pad readiness numbers, or a top sales rep fudging your forecast numbers to make it appear that you'll hit your quarterly goals, the long-term effects of lapses in integrity are dangerous.

CUTTING CORNERS NEVER LEADS TO EXCELLENCE.

Cutting corners never leads to excellence.

Integrity Leads to Trust

Rank and title don't necessarily give you the authority to lead; only the trust of the team you are leading can give you that ultimate authority. And how do you win that trust? By displaying integrity.

When subordinates—in the military or in the office—believe they lack support from above . . . when they see their leaders putting forth self-serving agendas or acting hypocritically . . . when they see careerism and hidden agendas . . . a trust gap comes into being.

Consider a study conducted by the Center for Creative Leadership to identify behaviors or traits that might predict the leadership success of top executives.[20] Senior managers and human resources executives identified twenty-one high-performing junior managers who had been promoted into middle management or executive positions and then failed to perform successfully. All these high performers had been on the fast track but then either were fired, retired early, or were never promoted again. So what happened?

When the researchers compared this group to twenty managers who did perform as expected and continued to advance in their careers, the biggest differentiator was this: Those who did not succeed were far more likely to have advanced their careers at the expense of others and to have broken promises or betrayed a trust. One example is an executive who didn't implement a simple policy change that had been promised and never gave his subordinates a reason. Although it was not a major policy change—there was no Enron-like collapse—the lack of change affected four levels of frustrated executives, managers, and individual contributors below him. In other words, their trust in the manager was now broken by a basic slip: not doing what he said he was going to do—not having integrity.

Declining trust is a huge and sweeping concern. According to an AP-GfK poll conducted in November 2013, Americans don't trust one another anymore.[21] These days only one-third of Americans say most people can be trusted; in 1972 the number was 50 percent.[22] Even the obnoxious gridlock and constant backbiting in politics might stem from the effects of an increasingly distrustful citizenry, according to April K. Clark, a Purdue University political scientist and public opinion researcher.[23] "It's like the rules of the game," Clark said. "When trust is low, the way we react and behave with each other becomes less civil."

Naturally, this same sentiment starts to infiltrate the workplace.

In a 2013 *Forbes* article, entrepreneur and author Glenn Llopis writes about employees' desire for more trustworthy and transparent leaders.[24] "They want to be informed of any change management efforts before—not after the fact," he says. And so managers must decide between "informing their employees of the entire truth and holding back certain realities so as not to unnecessarily scare people or lose top talent. More and more leaders today are being placed into uncomfortable moral dilemmas because they are attempting to salvage their own jobs while trying to maintain the trust and loyalty of their employees." Clearly, at times it can be tough to know what the right thing is. But integrity requires you to try.

If you want to earn your people's unconditional trust and the mandate to lead, make integrity a centerpiece of your leadership style. It's what fearless leaders do, and it's what you can do, too. Here are some ways to get started.

Be Authentic

When you're authentic, you're true to who you are. You'll never earn anyone's trust if you're a fake. Misdirection and shape-shifting may get you out of one or two tough leadership binds, but only when you learn to stay authentic will you excel in the leader's seat.

I talk about authenticity a lot, and sometimes people come up to me after a leadership training program and say something like, "What can I do to be more authentic?" Every time I hear it, I die a little bit inside. There's nothing you can *do* to make yourself more authentic. It's no good to represent yourself in a way that you hope makes you *look like* the real thing; you have to actually *be* the real thing. You can't slap on a veneer of authenticity and hope people like you more. In fact, that's the opposite of authenticity. You can't fake sincerity or just try to be charismatic. You have to really, truly care about your personal relationship with the people on the team. You have to be passionate about the mission and about where you're moving together.

If you can't muster actual enthusiasm about leading your team ahead, or if you feel you have to "put on" a persona to convince people that you're the real deal, it's probably time to step out of the game or pick a different lane. No amount of artifice or showmanship is going to get you there. True authenticity happens when a leader harnesses his or her sincere passion for leading and allows it to express itself in an individual way.

> ## YOU MUST FIRST BE WHO YOU REALLY ARE, THEN DO WHAT YOU NEED TO DO, IN ORDER TO HAVE WHAT YOU WANT.
>
> —MARGARET YOUNG

I think you can divide leaders into two groups: "takers" (the inauthentic leaders) and "givers" (authentic leaders). The takers are in it for themselves. They want you to support them so they can get more and get ahead, and they'll adopt whatever personality it takes to win you over. As long as the taker makes a lot of money or gains recognition, he or she could care less if the organization is successful; such individuals destroy much more value than they ever create. But oftentimes they don't get a lot of negative attention, because they appear to be powerful, charismatic people.

The givers, on the other hand, know that their role is to serve all their constituents—the stakeholders, the customers, the employees, the shareholders, the community. This is the kind of true authentic leader the world needs more of. These are the people who make really great things happen.

There are many ways to lead effectively, and a big part of authenticity is leading in a way that's true to you. As we've seen, you don't have to be a brash-and-brazen type to be a leader, nor do you have to possess the persuasive skills of Abraham Lincoln. You just have to follow a directive that is no less true for being a cliché: Be yourself. Be more like you!

Finding Your Own Style

Dolf van den Brink, president and chief executive of Heineken USA, speaks of how he learned this lesson about success and authenticity. He joined the company in his twenties, hoping to grow into a leadership role, and got his wish when, at age thirty-two, he was sent to the Congo to oversee a seven-hundred-person division whose market share and revenues were falling. He got off to a good start, calling everyone together and establishing five cultural values he'd developed after three weeks of touring the country. But he faltered as, following the advice of others, he tried to project an image of strength and authority that didn't feel natural. "I was thirty-two, and I probably looked twenty-eight, so I tried to behave and look older than I was," van den Brink says. Not only did the approach not win him the respect he was looking for, but the effort also exhausted the young leader.

Fortunately, van den Brink's wife stepped in with a piece of sage advice: "Just be yourself. Stop pretending." He took it to heart and started dressing more causally, letting himself be who he was.[25] The adjustment back to authenticity—and the trust it created—helped van den Brink effect an incredible turnaround for Heineken in the

Congo: By the time he left his division to become Heineken's US CEO, the division's market share had more than doubled, rising from 31 percent at the beginning of his tenure to 74.8 percent at the time of his exit.[26]

When you're fearless enough to be yourself as a leader, you free up a lot of time and energy. You stop obsessing about how you're coming across, and you have more of yourself, the good parts, to give your team. In the process, you win something priceless: the commitment of the people you're leading.

It can be uncomfortable to reveal your true self—it requires vulnerability and risks rejection—but when you suck it up and simply act like you, you avoid the far worse discomfort of being an ineffective leader. As you've probably seen in political debates, on TMZ, in the office, and even in your own neighborhood, there are a lot of people out there trying to emulate someone else—and they usually turn out to be jerks.

Fearless leaders can convey conviction without putting on a mask or adopting an attitude that isn't authentic. You must find your natural leadership style in order to soar. Otherwise, it's like walking around in a pair of tight shoes.

Unfortunately, many boards of directors are swayed by the charismatic qualities of hotshots who are looking to come in from the outside and save a company. Thanks to their good looks, charm, and personality, such would-be heroes persuade a lot of people to get behind them. But often, these folks end up doing more damage than anything else.

The outcome depends on whether charisma is matched by authenticity, whether style is backed by substance. If a leader is chosen for image rather than for character and integrity, then you will have a leader who doesn't do the job for the long term—someone who is all blow and no go.

This doesn't mean charisma is bad—it's actually great! Just don't think you can coast by on magnetism alone. You won't get real results if you're not putting forth the real you.

The Jet Doesn't Know the Difference

Women may face particular pressure to be something they're not when they take on a leadership role. As a female fighter pilot, I had to crash through cultural barriers and stereotypes to get my performance recognized, even though the jet I was flying clearly didn't care whether I was a man or a woman—it just needed the job done right. In this kind of situation, you have to conduct yourself with humility and grace. You can't afford to overreact to every inappropriate comment directed your way. You can, however, take control or ownership of the situation and redirect your comments in order to coach or educate misinformed coworkers in a respectful manner. Not everyone wishes you ill; sometimes they are simply unaware of how they're coming across.

You can't please everybody all the time; don't try to hide who you are or what you are passionate about. There's a fine line in behavior modification for women in a male-dominated environment. Determined not to be labeled an "emotional woman," I tried to maintain my bearing and not show too much emotion either way. Likewise, I tried not to be too bold or brash or to look like an "overbearing bitch." Did it work? Not so much. This was interpreted by some as a lack of passion on my part, which couldn't have been further from the truth. Authenticity as a pioneer was a true tightrope walk—very difficult when you are forging a path alone.

Three-quarters of the way through my F-14 training at the RAG (Replacement Air Group), I flew with an instructor who, at the end of a particularly challenging flight, told me that I reminded him of his wife—because I had polished nails and was polite, easy going, and pretty mild-mannered. He said that instead of the typical fighter guy, I was "perfect wife material"! This left me speechless—which is not an easy feat. We had just finished a flight in a $50 million combat aircraft. We had broken the sound barrier and intentionally departed controlled flight, which is actually a fairly violent experience. And yet here he sat, telling me he didn't see me as a fighter pilot, but as a wife. You've got to be kidding me! This was not the day I wanted to hear that. I wanted to unbuckle my harness, scramble to the back seat, and throttle him.

Instead, I said nothing: zilch, nada, zip. Why? Pure shock. How could I respond to such a goofy statement? First of all, he was my instructor, so he had positional authority over me. Second, I had heard a ton of trash before, and not much bothers me—maybe there was no hostile intent; maybe he was just clueless. Whatever the case, I had to maintain my integrity and authenticity despite this guy's perception of me—which was a *reality* to him. If I could do it over again, I'd have used that moment as a coaching opportunity. I could have worked to close that perception gap. Sometimes this can be as simple as speaking up. What I wish I would've said was "Damn skippy I will. But today? We're doing that fighter pilot thing . . . " A response like that—direct, with a bit of humor, allowing a "way out"—would have been my authentic response. Saying nothing? Ugh. I still regret it.

Just as in combat, in business things are not always equal. This concept took awhile for me to really come to grips with, although it's no secret that men and women are not always perceived as equals in the business world, particularly in male-dominated work environments. We can fight it, we can argue against it, and we can vow to change it, but we need to recognize this fact of life so that we know the framework in which we operate. Otherwise it's exhausting and not productive.

Learning how to fly the legendary F-14 Tomcat was a challenge in and of itself, but my time with the F-14 training squadron coincided with a very hostile, post-Tailhook environment. Investigations were ongoing into allegedly questionable behaviors and harassment by some intoxicated naval aviators in Las Vegas, and morale was low. The Navy was also trying to reduce its number of officers, and everybody was really frustrated by the cutbacks. Even though newly winged aviators were still being sent to the fleet as planned, there was the perception that women were taking the place of men—taking their flying slots—and the men didn't like it. In an environment of enormous hostility and paranoia, it didn't matter that I was qualified; I was female, which labeled me an outsider. When I first arrived at Naval Air Station Miramar, they didn't know what to do with me. I was like a new bear in the zoo.

So, added to the routine pressure of the job itself, there was this intense pressure of being a pioneer. I was always under the microscope. I was in a position where it was very tough to win the approval of a few of the folks—or to be seen as non-threatening—because of the backlash after the Navy suffered embarrassment over Tailhook. And, with very few other women as peers or in senior leadership positions, there was virtually no one to provide guidance or mentorship in this type of environment.

Although there were some fantastic instructors, there were times where I felt very much alone, and it took effort to remain authentic. It's a challenge when you know there are a handful of people who look at you with disregard, even disdain. This sort of scrutiny can paralyze your voice and squash your spirit. Not feeling heard, valued, or respected can shut you down and make you shy away from revealing your authentic self. For the most part, I managed to look inside myself and stay true to what I believed in, rather than trying to please the people around me or conform to their expectations.

It's something every leader has to do—man or woman, military or civilian. And it's not easy. It takes grit, commitment, and an unwavering belief that you have the ability to write your own story—and even that you have "permission" to do so. Too often we wait for an invitation to the party. We wait for acceptance and validation before we engage. But while you're waiting, someone else—someone who has the self-confidence to step up, who can manage their discomfort and pick themselves back up after a setback—is being promoted to your dream job.

Lead by Example

Although it is easy to talk about "doing the right thing," walking the walk can be challenging at times. But military officers must set the example for their troops in every aspect of their life—both on the battlefield and off. If they don't act with the integrity they expect from their team, how can they expect anyone to trust and follow them? This concept of "leading by example"—*Ductus exemplo* in Latin—is foundational to the training of US Navy officers; the motto is also prominently displayed at the United States Marine Corps Officer Candidate School.

Your team will be watching vigilantly for cues as to what you expect of them. When you lead with integrity, the message is clear; your words and actions are one and the same. As Einstein once said, "Setting an example is not the main means of influencing others; it is the only means." If you're not practicing what you preach—if you don't know your stuff, and if you aren't doing yourself what you expect of your team—you've lost the leadership game from the beginning. If you're telling them one thing and doing another, that's the exact opposite of integrity. You'll lose their respect, and productivity and morale will take a hit.

The character and integrity that you display sets the standard for your team. If your team sees you engaging in ethically questionable behavior, they may feel entitled to engage in similar behavior themselves. You're doing it, so why shouldn't they? So, if the CEO is overstating projected earnings, why wouldn't his or her salespeople overpromise and then underdeliver? Or call in sick, but actually go out golfing? When your team sees what you do, they'll feel comfortable doing that, too.

> **WHEN YOU LEAD WITH INTEGRITY, THE MESSAGE IS CLEAR; YOUR WORDS AND ACTIONS ARE ONE AND THE SAME.**

Too often we see in the press some CEO blathering on about how important his or her employees are and saying that they are "like family." And yet, with the wave of a hand, the CEO summarily dismisses thousands of loyal teammates and says there was "no choice." More often than not, a short time later we hear about the multimillion-dollar golden parachute these executives take as they leave the organization, moving on to pillage the next one. Or we hear about them receiving fat paychecks or even bonuses while their employee groups are suffering salary cuts or health benefit cuts. This is not fearless leadership, and it certainly is not leading with integrity.

Fearless leaders don't take, take, take while expecting their colleagues to give, give, give. Instead they share in the sacrifices of their team. If you expect your team to follow you to hell and back, you'd better lead with integrity and display the actions you want your team to mimic.

As both a female military officer and a former rower, I connect with the way Jennifer Dulski, president and COO of Change.org, describes this principle. She talks about how she took on her first leadership role in high school, when she became coxswain of the men's crew team. Surrounded by a bunch of guys, she would coach, steer, and strategize. Dulski's time as coxswain taught her a lot about leading: "You can't just come in and tell people what to do," she says. "You have to earn their trust, and, for me, that meant things like working out with them when we weren't in the boat. I did all the sprints on the beach. I did the stairs."[27] Dulski showed her team that she understood what was required of them and was willing to go through it herself.

Even small gestures toward solidarity with the people you lead go a long way toward showing them that you have integrity. I love one story about Rear Admiral Nora Tyson, the first woman in the US Navy to be named commander of a strike carrier group. Having had the opportunity to meet Rear Admiral Tyson, I was not surprised by the story that follows. She's smart, humble, and thoughtful, and she always puts mission before self. Just a few years ago, Tyson led a small delegation to Cambodia to plan the first significant training between the US Navy and the Royal Cambodian Navy. As Tyson and her companions went about their tour, the formal Cambodian Navy made a production out of each of Tyson's appearances, with "dozens of sailors lined up to render military honors."

At one point on the tour, the delegation got held up, and one such group of sailors ended up waiting for nearly two hours to greet Tyson and the rest of the delegation: about seventy men standing in sweltering tropical heat. Upon arrival, Tyson and the others were ushered past the line of men and into a pleasantly cool conference room.

But Tyson understood the negative message this would send to the sailors, so she walked back out of the conference room, retreading the thirty yards to the beginning of the formation, and worked her way back, shaking each sailor's hand and expressing her gratitude for the greeting. "The sailors were shocked," wrote Lieutenant Commander Mike Morley, who attended the gathering. "They rarely if ever receive such favorable attention from their own senior officers, let alone from a foreigner."[28]

What a great way to show integrity! As you guide your team, be constantly on the lookout for ways to prove to your team that you personally do everything you require of them. This type of leadership by example is so much more important than impressing any of your own higher-ups. As Admiral Thomas Moorer, former chief of naval operations, once said, "Young officers should not spend their time trying to impress seniors. On the contrary, they should spend their time trying to impress those that work for them. They are the ones [who] make them look good."[29]

Today's business environment is hypercompetitive and rapidly changing. Leaders face many different leadership challenges. This reality makes integrity and leading by example all the more critical.

Your Troops Eat First

I once had a commanding officer who was lauded for having more arrested carrier landings—"traps"— in the F-14 Tomcat than anyone else. He even bragged about it. At the same time, most of the new, young aviators in his squadron were barely getting enough landings to stay current and proficient—to remain safe, in other words. This is not leadership by example; this is looking out for Number One.

In business as in the military, you are getting paid to look after your people: your teammates, your customers, your employees, your shareholders, and your clients. That's your obligation, your responsibility. When people are committed to the team, even risking their lives and livelihoods, and you shortchange them—that's irresponsible. Fearless leadership means it is no longer just about you. It doesn't matter whether you are leading the most talented, high-performing team in the world or your team appears to be short on talent—your job as a fearless leader must be to bring out the best in your people. It is about getting your *team* aboard the ship safely, about getting your *team* across the finish line together. If you're looking out for your own power, fame, and money, that's just plain wrong, and it won't serve you—or anyone else—in the long run.

Take your cue from Evan Wittenberg, the head of Global Leadership Development at Google, Inc. When asked, "What is the biggest mistake a leader can make?" he said, "Betraying trust. It's something that is very valued in the relationship between leaders and everybody else, and if you break that one—nothing else matters."[30] Always put your people first. *Always.*

ALWAYS PUT YOUR PEOPLE FIRST. *ALWAYS.*

A great example of why employees learn to loathe executives comes from none other than American Airlines. Back in 2003, then-CEO Don Carty threatened bankruptcy to all the employees unless they gave up $1.8 billion in wage concessions. He begged for these concessions as a "shared sacrifice" necessary to keep the company afloat, but he failed to tell them that he was concurrently handing out *millions of dollars* in retention bonuses to the executive team. To make matters worse (if that's possible), he also set up a protected, irrevocable trust for the organization's top forty-five executives, guaranteeing their pensions.[31]

Unfortunately this pattern of asking for concessions from employee groups while feathering the nests of management has continued. In 2012 Hostess, maker of the legendary Twinkie, cut employee pay 8 percent while management received millions in bonuses—*while the company was in bankruptcy.*[32] In early 2014 Barclays bank cut 12,000 employees while increasing manager bonuses 10 percent.[33] None of these high-powered executives put their people first—a leadership and management failure. Although some American Airlines employees continue to work hard while having every reason to be perturbed with management, this leadership choice has not benefited AA in the long run; their employee groups are disengaged, and customer service appears to have suffered.

You might say that your troops or your employees are the most important thing, or that flight safety is your most important value, but if your actions don't match your words, you will lose the trust and confidence of your crew. If you claim that your people are the most important thing while in reality you are protecting your own self-interests first (and only then, if it's convenient, looking after the others), why on earth would you ever expect them to respect and follow you? Perhaps more important for the business, how can leaders who put themselves first expect their employees to put the customer first?

Putting your teammates and employees first is smart leadership. After all, they are the main value of your organization. Without them, you are alone and will never truly be successful.

One of the first things you learn going through military officer training is this principle: *Your troops eat first.* Leaders with integrity always keep their troops in mind. They eat last. They take care of their employees and teammates before they take care of themselves.

In earlier times, this was simply a survival technique: First the horses were fed, then the soldiers, and then the officers. Over time, it was shortened to simply, "The troops eat first." This motto is just as relevant today as it was then, though for different reasons. In the corporate world, it simply means, "Take care of your people."

One of the biggest mistakes you can make as a leader is to put your self-interest ahead of the best interest of your team, of the organization that you lead. I share this with C-level leaders because it's not a perspective they hear often (no one ever wants to tell the emperor he has no clothes). Leadership is not about titles, positions, or glory. The best kind of leadership is about setting an example; it's about influence, integrity, inspiration, and courage

Frederick W. Smith, a former USMC captain, is the founder, chairman, president, and CEO of FedEx, a Fortune 100 company. Originally known as Federal Express, it was the first overnight express delivery company in the world and is now the largest. Fred Smith has a lot to say about leadership and putting people first:

> The greatest leadership principle I learned in the Marine Corps was the necessity to take care of the troops in a high-performance-based organization.
>
> The Marine Corps' strong emphasis on this overriding leadership requirement has been of inestimable importance to me in developing FedEx over the years. In the main, people want to be committed to an organization and to do a good job. The principles of leadership taught by the USMC, and based on two centuries of experience, will produce outstanding organizational results in any setting, if those principles are studiously followed. In short, FedEx owes its success to this simple truth.
>
> Talent is not enough.[34]

As a leader, you build trust each time you put the team's needs above your own—each time you choose integrity over title, honor over personal comfort, and truth over expediency. Fearless leaders keep their word and live up to promises made. Over time, your influence as a leader becomes much more difficult to sustain, and soon enough your followers will be few. If you fail to abide by this philosophy, eventually your team will leave. Your organization's survival depends on your ability to form trusting relationships—to always put the troops first.

You must earn the right to be a leader. Your credibility is your leadership currency. With it, you are in the black. Without it, you are bankrupt.

If you want to be a fearless leader—and I don't care if we're talking C-suite, VP, bank manager, plant manager, sales rep, or individual contributor—you must really hold yourself accountable for your actions and your team's success. For example, in 2013 Apple CEO Tim Cook announced that he would forfeit up to one-third of his compensation if Apple's stock underperformed relative to other S&P 500 companies. This means that he could lose up to $130 million over the term of his employment contract. How's that for having skin in the game? It's a powerful example of leadership integrity and of how a leader can demonstrate that the team's performance and well-being come before his or her own personal interests.

Make the Right Calls, Even When It Hurts

In his commencement speech at Saint Anselm College, Tyco International CEO Dennis Kozlowski said, "You will be confronted with questions every day that test your morals. . . . Think carefully and, for your sake, do the right thing."[35] Seventeen days later,

Kozlowski was indicted for tax evasion. Hardly an example of walking the talk.

Although accountability makes some people uncomfortable, I'm a big fan. Fearless leaders always hold themselves responsible for doing the right thing, even when it means standing up to pressure, being a thorn in someone's side, or inconveniencing themselves. As goody-two-shoes as that may sound, fearlessly following your moral compass is absolutely vital to earning your team's trust and leading effectively.

Because they're committed to doing what's right, fearless leaders have a low "drift factor," as an aviator would say. In other words, they have a tendency to stay on the straight course. They aren't afraid of making the right call. They know that they have to be the ones to speak up when they see something wrong. They lead with very consistent values and with their hearts as well as their heads. This is a lot harder than it sounds, especially when you factor in the seduction of making a lot of money by deviating just a little bit from your values.

FEARLESS LEADERS ALWAYS HOLD THEMSELVES RESPONSIBLE FOR DOING THE RIGHT THING, EVEN WHEN IT MEANS STANDING UP TO PRESSURE, BEING A THORN IN SOMEONE'S SIDE, OR INCONVENIENCING THEMSELVES.

When Leonard Roberts became CEO of fast-food restaurant chain Arby's, it was losing money. He is credited with turning the company around and making Arby's profitable. But when Arby's ownership leveled vicious personal attacks at board members, threatening to withhold bonuses for Roberts's staff and to deny promised help to Arby's franchisees in order to further increase profits, Roberts resigned from the board of directors. "I knew what I had to do," he said later. "I had to take a stand, so I resigned from the board."[36]

In retaliation for his stand, Arby's ownership fired Roberts.

What happened to Leonard Roberts after this experience? Do you think he slinked off to lick his wounds? Did he consider himself a failure?

Nope.

He joined another restaurant chain—Shoney's—as chairman and CEO. After he was hired, however, he found out that Shoney's was the subject of the largest racial discrimination lawsuit in history.

Although Roberts resolved to settle this suit without long-term impact, it proved even more challenging than he had imagined: The Shoney's owner refused to hire African Americans and had a history of firing any restaurant manager who did. The company owner eventually agreed to pay up but demanded the new CEO's resignation. Roberts had now lost his two jobs in two years.

"My stand on integrity was getting a little hard on my wife and kids," Roberts admitted. "However, I knew it had to be done. There was no other way." Here is an executive who knows it isn't enough to just talk about integrity; as a fearless leader you have to *live* it.

It should come as no surprise, then, that Roberts landed on his feet, becoming CEO of Radio Shack and, a year later, CEO of parent company Tandy Corporation. Today, Roberts says, "You cannot fake it. You must stand up for what is right regardless . . . You cannot maintain your integrity 90 percent and be a leader. It's got to be 100 percent."[37]

You can't be a fearless leader, a high performer, if you are afraid of losing your job. Sometimes you must make the tough calls. And your teammates and employees are always watching to see whether you are making the right calls or merely covering your six—your backside, your six o'clock, your rear.

A lack of integrity can also be found when leaders (be they politicians, CEOs, VPs, managers, or shift bosses) just say what others want to hear—when all you hear is "Yes, sir," "Yes, ma'am," and "Everything is great here." This bootlicker mentality is corrosive at best and destructive at worst. In an environment where only the people who never rock the boat get promoted, the folks who actually dare to raise their hands and tell the emperor he has no clothes are goners. They're painted as disloyal rabble-rousers.

What are those people who stand up to the situation likely to hear? "If you can't get this job done, I'll find someone else who will," or "Hmmm, I'm not sure if you're a 'team player'." When you encounter this situation, you must decide how badly you want to be a fearless leader. Compromising your integrity just to keep your job is not the path that will take you there.

Making the big leadership decisions based on your moral compass rather than what's in your personal best interest will shove you out of your comfort zone fast. And remember—that's a good thing. As a fearless leader, you thrive outside your comfort zone. You run toward discomfort, because you know it makes you better. And with every honorable decision you make—whether it's taking accountability for your personal and professional growth rather than playing office politics to get promoted . . . stating sales forecast numbers accurately instead of what you think your manager wants to hear . . . or simply telling a customer, "I'm sorry we made a mistake. How can we make this right?"—you strengthen your integrity and your team's faith in you. Profits and power are temporary. Great relationships with people who trust you? They're forever.

I tell you this because you *will* face adversity and temptation at times, and those experiences will introduce you to yourself. They will challenge you. When you are in a leadership position and you choose not to stand up and make the tough calls, to get in there and get your nose bloodied, the team you're in charge of starts to become schizophrenic. They don't know what to do or whom to trust. They don't know if you will have their backs when the chips are down—and if they're unsure, that's probably because you won't. So your teammates no longer know if you are trustworthy or even what you stand for. They're on their own. And that doesn't normally end well.

Former president and famed general Dwight Eisenhower famously stated, "The supreme quality for leadership is unquestionably integrity. Without it, no real success is possible." In business as in the military, people just want the truth, and they want to be led by someone who stands up for the truth—someone who doesn't turn into a limp-cheese weasel when confronted with adversity. When leaders slip into desperate survival mode and are scrambling at the helm of a sinking ship, trust is one of the first things to fall overboard. But leadership without mutual respect and trust is a contradiction in terms. Be careful to follow your moral compass so you won't let your team down.

Admit Your Mistakes

Every great leader takes risks, and every great leader fails sometimes. That's because these individuals display the first trait of fearless leaders: courage. They push aside their fear of failure and use the second fearless trait, tenacity, to go for it anyway. When the occasional, inevitable flop happens, it signals a perfect opportunity to display the third trait of fearless leaders—integrity—by admitting the failure openly.

The absolute last thing you want to do is BS the troops. It may get you off easy (in other words, keep you in the comfort zone), but it makes you look terrible in front of your people. Because, trust me, your team *will* know when you're bullshitting them. When you try to stretch the truth (or cover it up), you also run the risk of dragging your team's reputation into the gutter, which would tarnish others' perception of both you and your organization.

EVERY GREAT LEADER TAKES RISKS, AND EVERY GREAT LEADER FAILS SOMETIMES.

Say you are the manufacturer of a clothing item that turns out to be see-through, and you go on television blaming the consumers, saying their body type is wrong or they're too heavy. After the PR firestorm, would you have a change of heart a week later—and the guts to go back on air a week later and apologize to your customers? To take responsibility? Or say you were wrong with a capital *W*? Do you have the integrity and fearlessness to course-correct and be transparent with your team and your customers about what happened? Or will you do what human nature pushes you to do: try to blame someone else or sweep it under the rug before anyone notices? The problem is that someone on your team *will* notice. And by not addressing the issue head-on, you have broken that trust.

Admitting your mistakes also serves as a way to lead by example. If your team members see you displaying the intestinal fortitude required to take risks and then be honest when things don't work out, they'll be encouraged to do the same in their own work and in their own lives.

Avoiding blame is often a blind spot for top-level profession-als, military leaders, executives, and others. There is a very fine line between a confident leader and an arrogant one; confidence inspires and attracts people, whereas arrogance can make leaders unapproach-able. Rarely do arrogant leaders get the unvarnished truth or hon-est feedback from the troops, direct reports, or coworkers that could save them from a misstep or embarrassment. Oftentimes their orga-nization's profitability and reputations quickly get dragged to the ocean floor.

Examples abound of so-called leaders who failed to own up to their mistakes: Senator John Edwards and campaign finance law vio-lations. Ponzi schemes run by Bernie Madoff and Allen Stanford. Executives at Lehman Brothers responsible for failed sub-prime mort-gage lending practices. Top athletes in (insert your favorite sport here) busted for illegal performance-enhancing drugs. It's not an exhaustive list, but clearly no one is immune when it comes to our instinct to avoid accountability.

Too often we base our actions on the question *What will people think?* rather than making a decision seated firmly in our values. If you've made one of those mistakes, it's best to go with your gut, admit the mistake, and move on quickly. You stand to lose a lot as a leader by choosing not to do so, and one of the first casualties will be the trust of your followers. Conversely, as your team realizes you are willing to step up and make a tough call instead of taking an easy way out, trust will actually grow.

Babe Didrikson Zaharias was one of America's most decorated all-around athletes, a champion amateur golfer in the 1932 Olympics and later a professional golfer. As the story goes, she once penalized herself two strokes after accidentally playing the wrong ball. "Why did you do it?" asked a friend. "No one saw you. No one would have known the difference."

"I would have known," replied Babe Zaharias, a guardian of integrity.[38]

Sweeping issues under the rug or trying to hide mistakes is not helpful to your business or to your goal of becoming a fearless leader. In fact, the opposite is typically true: Both individuals and organizations can benefit when they see the value in admitting their mistakes. Big IT companies and other private tech companies like Facebook, Google, and Microsoft routinely seek out people to find bugs or glitches in their products—and sometimes even pay them thousands of dollars to do so. Fearless leaders want to know the issues they need to confront.

Instead of shirking your next misstep to avoid embarrassment, why not embrace it? Run toward the fear, own the mistake, and be vulnerable in front of your team. Often this not only proves your integrity but also brings the team together. In her latest book, *Daring Greatly*, Dr. Brené Brown, a research professor at the University of Houston College of Social Work, talks about the power of vulnerability. In a response to a student, she explained, "The unwillingness to engage with the vulnerability of not knowing often leads to making excuses, dodging the question, or worst-case scenario—bullshitting. That's the deathblow of any relationship."

A true leader can't react in fear when trying to make decisions. When people feel afraid, vulnerable, or threatened, they tend to make terrible decisions. They very quickly go into CYA ("cover your ass") mode. So, how do you make the right decisions when faced with a challenging situation? Start by asking yourself, *What do I believe?*

I still believe in the Navy's core values: honor, courage, and commitment. Every day I work hard to be a little bit better at those three values than I was the day before.

Life will constantly be testing you—your commitment to the thing you say matters most to you. Talking about integrity at the dinner table, in meetings, and with your kids is a great first step toward strengthening your integrity muscles. But acting with integrity—remaining aligned with your goals, staying authentic, serving those you lead—that is your true challenge. Integrity—it can't be bought or sold, but it can be lost quickly.

Now you have a working knowledge of the fundamental elements of fearless leadership—courage, tenacity, integrity. Next we'll step back and look at those principles in action.

PART II: FEARLESS LEADERSHIP IN ACTION

Chapter 4

VISION

PAINTING A BOLD, INSPIRING VIEW OF THE FUTURE

*If your actions inspire others to dream more, learn more, do more,
and become more, you are a leader.*
—*John Quincy Adams*

What do fearless leaders do, day in and day out, to marshal their people and lead the whole team to a better place than where it began? There's no question in my mind: A fearless leader begins the work of leadership with a bold vision.

The vision you create and hand down to your people is going to be the cornerstone of the team's success. It all starts with a clear concept, a view of where you want to go. If your vision is limited, your potential and possibilities are too.

The very essence of leadership is the ability to create a picture of success and bring people toward it. Your vision gives the team a universal understanding of who you are, as both an individual and a leader within the organization; who they are as members of the team;

and where the whole group is headed. It's a chart to your destination, providing a steady compass to orient your team. And when the seas get rough, the vision allows you to navigate the challenges and come out ahead.

Of course, coming up with a vision and setting it as the benchmark for yourself and everyone under you isn't a cakewalk. It puts you on the line; it tests your ability to inspire people. And by telling people exactly what you want for the team, you set yourself up to fall short if the vision isn't met. So, like everything else a great leader does, creating a vision requires fearlessness and accountability. But just because this task feels intimidating doesn't mean you can shirk it. If you don't have the *courage* to set the vision, the *tenacity* to keep after it, and the *integrity* to pursue it authentically, your team is going to be dead in the water.

IF YOU DON'T HAVE THE *COURAGE* TO SET THE VISION, THE *TENACITY* TO KEEP AFTER IT, AND THE *INTEGRITY* TO PURSUE IT AUTHENTICALLY, YOUR TEAM IS GOING TO BE DEAD IN THE WATER.

Trying to lead without a vision in place is like trying to build a house without a blueprint: You're going to waste a ton of time and money, and you'll probably end up with a rickety structure. But when you have that blueprint—a vision of who you are and where you want to be, and where you want the organization to be, in the future—your chances of developing the right strategy greatly improve.

As we'll see in this chapter, clear vision is not just wishful thinking. It's more than simply imagining what you hope the future will be. It's an incredible tool that catalyzes your team, gives it purpose and focus, sustains it in challenging times, and helps it perform at the highest level. You and your team have to be able to see yourself accomplishing that dream without losing your way or getting distracted. The right vision can make that possible.

What Does Success Look Like?

The top of an aircraft carrier is the world's most unforgiving, dangerous industrial worksite. When you're launching planes at close to 200 miles per hour from a steel flight deck seven stories above the waterline, having a clear vision matters. With an average age of nineteen—mostly fresh out of high school—my carrier's crew had a complex and risky set of tasks to perform, so our vision had to be vivid and compelling enough to unify and motivate us. And that it did. Our vision of success was simple: We wanted to safely launch and recover airplanes—twenty-four hours a day, seven days a week, 365 days a year. We wanted to bring every pilot who left the deck back in one piece and to bring everyone on that aircraft carrier home. There's no "going through the motions" in this type of environment. You have to be onboard with the vision and allow it to drive your every action.

On the carrier, with clarity of vision and purpose, we all knew what success looked like and understood the role we each played in making it a reality. Whether your team is launching planes, installing routers, switches, and feeds, or selling toothpaste, it's imperative that you, as a leader, step up and provide the vision that empowers the team to achieve high performance. Our inspiring vision is the fuel that allows common people like us to attain uncommon results. In aviation, just as in business, we may not have chosen one another as teammates, but we can all get focused on doing one thing and doing it well.

I've worked with many corporate clients, and I've seen a lot of confusion among the concepts of *vision, mission,* and *purpose.* Before we get on with more ideas for how you can create and implement a vision for your team, let's get specific on our terminology. For me, the essence of *vision* is the picture of the desired future. It's the dream, the big goal. It's specific and motivating. It inspires action.

Mission, on the other hand, hits on the same ideas but is more focused on action. It's what you're doing to get there. For our purposes here, *mission is part of the vision.* Even so, keep in mind that you don't want to cram strategies and tactics into the vision, as this confuses your people and waters down the message. (And we'll be covering how to prepare and perform later, in chapter 6.)

Finally, *purpose* refers to the "why" part of what your team is doing. This is absolutely critical. If your people don't have a great and personally resonant reason for doing what they're doing, the whole team will flounder. For me, purpose is the byproduct of a great vision, and later in this chapter we'll see how vision creates purpose and why that's so important in a high-performing team.

Now, let's look at how you can paint a picture of a successful future and get your people focused on getting there.

Own Your Role as the Catalyst

The first thing to realize is that vision starts with you, the leader. *You* are the catalyst—the person who steps up with a bold vision that changes everything for the team. You have to put it out there and be personally responsible for championing it. That doesn't mean you don't listen to others' ideas or take constructive criticism on where the team is going. But you have to realize that *you* are the catalyst for getting your team moving toward the vision. *You* are the one who can move the performance needle and help your team break through the noise, chaos, and competing priorities of today's challenging environment. You can't get bogged down in the day-to-day and hope that the vision magically comes together or coalesces out of the ether. You can't wait for an invitation to put forth your bold vision. You have to hammer it out,

YOU ARE THE CATALYST FOR GETTING YOUR TEAM MOVING TOWARD THE VISION.

present it proudly, and be the spark that gets people excited about it. Everybody has visions of the future, but not many are able to clearly articulate to others what they see—or to explain why it is important and exciting.

One of the greatest challenges in the complex and ambiguous environment of leadership is to get clarity on what you want your team to accomplish. A fuzzy idea that comes from the top will not get any clearer further down the line. Stephen Covey, esteemed businessman and bestselling author of *The Seven Habits of Highly Effective People*, states, "Begin with the end in mind." Ask yourself the question we touched on above: *What will success look like?* If you can answer this, you'll have a fighting chance of getting your team aligned to your vision.

Thinking big about the future and sharing your vision with the team can be scary, but fearless leaders do it every day. They do it because they know that without a vision, their team's efforts will be scattershot and uncoordinated. People will grow frustrated and distracted. They'll spin their wheels without getting anywhere. They may even work at cross-purposes to one another.

But if your people have a great vision in front of them, they'll actually be excited about showing up to work. They'll feel that the part they play serves something greater than themselves. Just as you need a vision of success to keep you moving forward tenaciously on your leadership trajectory (think back to those pilot's wings in the shadow box), your team needs that lodestar to follow—a bright, invigorating mental picture of what the future holds. When that's in place, you and your team will be able to master complexity, handle constant and rapid change, and go farther faster.

As the catalyst, you need to spark people's dreams and desires. You're the person who can come into a room and get the team aligned and excited so you can all get where you want to go. The vision isn't a plan, a strategy, or a series of steps—it's the inspiration behind those things. As others have pointed out, Martin Luther King Jr. gave the "I Have a Dream" speech, not the "I Have a Plan" speech. Your vision should resonate with the team emotionally, and it should get them pumped about what lies ahead. It doesn't have to say how you're going to get there; it just has to say what it'll look like when you do.

Fearless leaders also deliver their vision with sincere enthusiasm and an infectious attitude. Communicating a vision statement with the emotional impact of a bored TSA inspector is not inspiring—your people will have zero emotional connection with the goal. You can't just go through the motions. You have to be the one who causes that chemical reaction, who energizes the team. Ask questions; learn details about your teammates. You have to make them excited about the infinite possibilities of the future.

Help People Focus

The number one benefit of a vision is that it gives everyone focus. And the clearer the vision, the greater the focus you'll create among the team—and the more momentum you'll have behind you. Your challenge as a leader is to cast a vision so clear that everybody on your team—everybody in management, every individual contributor—is able to see the future the way you see the future and is able to home in on precisely what it will take to get there.

If you are going to succeed as a leader and as a team, creating a focal point is more crucial than ever. Distractions today are abundant. We get pulled in a thousand different directions constantly. A recent study published by Duke University that followed Generation X children discovered that the ability to concentrate, to focus, and to ignore distractions was the biggest predictor of success.[39] This ability to focus was an even bigger factor than IQ or the socioeconomic status of the family you grew up in. Just as a child's ability to focus is a predictor of his or her success later in life, your team's ability to focus is a predictor of its success down the road. And what's the number one way to build that focus? By starting with a clear, inspiring vision.

There is an enormous amount of competition vying for your team's attention. In order to remain relevant, you need to cut through the noise to gain and hold your teammates' attention. As a leader, you must think about those things that do not contribute to the end state. If it doesn't support your goals, get rid of it! As we say in fighter aviation, "If you lose sight, you lose the fight."

The clearer the vision, the easier it is to say no to those things that don't help you achieve your goals. That vision decides for you. It cuts out the unnecessary and imposes beneficial limitations. It helps you and the team focus on what matters.

Will It Make the Boat Go Faster?

I owe an early lesson in focusing on what matters to my time on the rowing team at the University of Wisconsin. Rowing is a grueling sport, often ranked as one of the top three most difficult on earth. Everything about it hurts. In fact, it is sometimes described as the only sport that started off as capital punishment. Seriously! In southern Europe, starting in the 1400s, if you were convicted of a crime, you were either executed or sentenced to be an oarsman.

Thanks to Mother Nature, the best water—the flattest—is usually early in the morning, so 5:00 a.m. wakeups are the norm. And when you are rowing at a competitive level, the pain of getting out of bed in the cold predawn is only the beginning. Maintaining physical coordination in this effort is critical. One misplaced "catch"—dipping your oar in the water—could launch you from the boat. Your hands look as if they've been put through a meat grinder: blisters, calluses, blisters under calluses. Your legs feel as though a million needles are jammed in them. You're sure that either your lungs will explode or you will suffocate from lack of oxygen—whichever comes first. The pain is so intense it scrambles your thinking; every bit of survival logic is telling you to quit. Even your eyes are affected by the effort—your vision goes full-on tunnel. You are convinced you might die. You're sure there is no way in hell you'll ever make it to the finish line, and yet . . . There is the voice inside your head, just loud enough, that tells you not to quit on your teammates. So you focus. You persist.

The summer before my junior year of college, a group of us rowers stayed at school for the summer session. We took a couple of classes, and we trained for the fall racing season. In particular, we were preparing for a prestigious race in Boston—the Head of the Charles—that draws top national and international rowing crews along with hundreds of thousands of spectators annually. No one outside of our team expected our crew from UW to do well, and for a few fairly legitimate reasons. First, we were a young crew; we had a gap in experience and seniority. Second, there were upwards of forty-five other crews in our one race alone. And third, one of them had just rowed in the Olympics. Seriously? What were our chances?

As a leader—seasoned college junior that I was—I had learned already the power of establishing an end state, a vision to which everybody could orient their day-to-day decision making. I knew there had to be a catalyzing or compelling idea that would get our people headed in the right direction. The vision here was simple: We wanted to win at the Head of the Charles. All we had to do was make our boat faster than the other boats. Ahem . . . So every day that summer we asked ourselves as we were training, "Will this make the boat go faster?" Everything that we did was in the context of answering that basic question.

If we were going to run stadium stairs, would an extra fifteen minutes make the boat go faster? To our discomfort, manifested in the immense pain we experienced in those fifteen minutes, yes, it would; it *had to*, because this was hard. We would grind out excruciating workouts day after day with a singular goal in mind: winning at the Head of the Charles. Most days it would've been easier to stop.

As all of our friends and pals were ramping up for their nightly college activities, we would have to ask ourselves, "Will this make the boat go faster?" Of course, we came to that answer quickly: No, it wouldn't. Now, I'm not saying I never went out—I did go to the University of Wisconsin after all! But I knew, as did my teammates, that how we conducted ourselves socially and the choices we made would directly affect our ability to move the boat faster—to be successful.

We showed up at the Head of the Charles that October, and our boat swung through that three-mile course with grit, power, practiced precision, and a fierce but quiet determination. At the end of the race, when all finish race times were in, we were number one: the top collegiate crew in the nation.

We accomplished this because we kept our vision out front. We were willing to do the hard work required. We held on to a defined picture of the future, and we stayed focused on what matters.

When you know what your end state is, you can make the best decisions to accomplish your goal. You must be deliberate and disciplined, because there will certainly be challenges and setbacks along the way. But when we went to practice rowing, we had a goal in mind: What are the things we need to do as a team to make the boat go faster? How do I need to behave as an individual to make the boat go faster? And then we took action. We did the work; we pursued that goal no matter the obstacles. Because we had that end state to reflect on and weigh against, we had a decision-making filter. Our shared vision was a sort of guardrail that kept us from going off course, and it shaped what we did not only in practice but also away from practice. The lessons I learned from my time at UW—about persistence, grit, and the power of possibility—stay with me to this day.

A CLEAR VISION GIVES PEOPLE FOCUS, AND FOCUS IS POWER. DILUTED FOCUS EQUALS DILUTED POWER.

The big takeaway here is this: A clear vision gives people focus, and focus is power. Diluted focus equals diluted power. So a clear vision must always come first. *Always.* No matter how much time we spend developing a strategic plan, if the vision is not clear, the strategy will not matter. It will be ineffective. As a leader, you should think carefully about those things that do not contribute to the end state—and throw them overboard. Get rid of the noise.

Focus to Survive

The US military understands the power of vision and focus—and how crucial these things are in the most adverse of circumstances. That's why it provides a training program—its most advanced—that is not often talked about in civilian circles: Survival, Evasion, Resistance, and Escape (SERE) school. Located in several different areas of the country, SERE school is attended mostly by military aircrew and special operations personnel who are considered to be at high risk for capture. It's here that I encountered an incredible vision of what it means to conduct yourself honorably when captured by the enemy—and learned how to maintain the intense focus required to do so.

I was fortunate to attend SERE school in Southern California with a select group of other naval aviators, recon Marines, Navy SEALs, Marine Corps snipers, and Navy special warfare combatant-craft crewmembers. This intensive training course has two parts: classroom and in the field. The classroom work lasted about a week and included a great deal of history, lessons learned from previous POWs, and how to share just enough information with a captor to stay alive and yet not betray your country. The second phase is conducted in the field under extreme conditions and encompasses those basic skills necessary for survival in hostile environments anywhere in the world: how to not only survive, but then evade capture by hostile forces. To increase your chances of survival if and when you are captured, you are given comprehensive resistance training in a full immersion, realistic environment. This is not for the faint of heart.

The SERE school trains soldiers to do our best to live up to the military's Code of Conduct. The code embodies well-established, time-honored American values, and it emerged as a response to the lack of preparation of our soldiers in the Korean War. Suffering under horrifying, inhumane torture, too many POWs experienced profound physical and psychological damage.

The Code of Conduct has six articles, and all soldiers are now expected to live up to them while in combat or captivity. Together, they represent a powerful vision, a very specific picture that showed us what to focus on should we, God forbid, ever end up as POWs. Here are the six articles, which we all had memorized:

1. I am an American, fighting in the forces that guard my country and our way of life. I am prepared to give my life in their defense.

2. I will never surrender of my own free will. If in command, I will never surrender the members of my command while they still have the means to resist.

3. If I am captured, I will continue to resist by all means available. I will make every effort to escape and aid others to escape. I will accept neither parole nor special favors from the enemy.

4. If I become a prisoner of war, I will keep the faith with my fellow prisoners. I will give no information nor take part in any action that might be harmful to my comrades. If I am senior, I will take command. If not, I will obey the lawful orders of those appointed over me and will back them up in every way.

5. When questioned, should I become a prisoner of war, I am required to give name, rank, service number, and date of birth. I will evade answering further questions to the utmost of my ability. I will make no oral or written statements disloyal to my country and its allies or harmful to their cause.

6. I will never forget that I am American, fighting for freedom, responsible for my actions, and dedicated to the principles that made my country free. I will trust in my God and in the United States of America.

In the second phase of training, we had to put this code to the test. After traveling some ninety miles from Naval Air Station Coronado out to the mountains of Warner Springs, it was time for the immersion to begin. As we got off the buses, they broke us up into separate teams of eight and then further into pairs. Outfitted with not much more than a compass, a map, a knife, and a signal mirror, we roamed the first couple of days through the scrubby California hillside day and night, looking for food and water while practicing land navigation, concealment, shelter building, tracking, and animal trapping skills. This place wasn't exactly lush pickings; anything that may have been edible was eaten a long time ago. But there was plenty of tall, dead grass, which gave you something to chew on. Nights were spent trying to stay warm. The mountains of California get pretty chilly after sundown, and the only to make it through the night without chipping a tooth was to line up like a family of sardines in a can. So we did. No room for rank or gender under the moonlight; this was all about staying warm.

As you can imagine, with no food and limited water for a group of fit twenty-two to twenty-five-year-old individuals, tempers were flaring and moods were cranky by about day three. Suddenly one of our instructor-trainers appeared with a little, fluffy white rabbit. And two carrots. The carrots were not to feed the bunny.

More instruction on survival techniques was passed along. This part wasn't new to me, since my dad was a Marine and we grew up learning some of these skills. But for a couple of guys, the woods-to-roasting-stick process was just a little too graphic to stomach. (Okay by me—one bunny doesn't go too far, anyway.)

It was now time to start the evasion phase. The rules were straightforward: Don't get caught. If you did, you would get extra time spent as a POW. After a certain amount of time had passed, the evasion phase would be over and a loud horn would sound. If you hadn't already been captured, you were to find the nearest road and wait to turn yourself in.

I was paired up with a younger Marine recon guy from Georgia—two years younger. I could tell he was a little pissed that he had been paired up with a female. That's okay. What he didn't know, yet, was that my dad had spent countless hours traipsing around 250 acres of woods in northern Wisconsin with my brother and me, equipped with nothing but a whistle and a compass. The young Marine thrust the map at me and said, "You think you can handle this?"

"No problem," I replied, quietly thanking Dad. Clearly, there was no advantage found in spending additional time in the POW camp. Our common goal was to make it to the horn blast. We did. In fact, we were the last ones to come into camp.

And then the resistance training began. This is the part of SERE training not often talked about, and I won't go into great detail here regarding the actual techniques used. Suffice it to say the techniques used to push us to our limits were not any different from what you or I read about in the papers. Waterboarding, small boxes, sleep deprivation, nakedness, cold showers, physical interference, solitary confinement—you name it, it's all there. The goal of the training was to push you to your absolute limit without causing long-term physical damage. The military was trying to impart to us the lessons learned the extremely hard way by the POWs imprisoned at, for example, the Hanoi Hilton in North Vietnam. What information (past name, rank, service number, and date of birth) do you share to avoid execution—while also avoiding the betrayal of your country and of your fellow POWs' confidence? How do you survive in a way that will allow you to return home with honor? The focus was to survive while abiding by the Code of Conduct. Those who didn't make it through the course were transferred out of their current high-risk assignments.

Perhaps one of the most poignant, extreme examples of focusing on what matters comes from Admiral James Stockdale and his POW experience during the Vietnam War. Remember, one of the main tenets of our Code of Conduct is that if captured, you are never to give up any more information than your name, rank, birth date, and service number. After assuming the position of senior ranking officer in one of the POW camps, Admiral Stockdale soon realized that he and the other POWs would eventually break under the extreme torture and probably would violate at least part of the Code of Conduct, risking not only disgrace but also a broken, unrecoverable spirit.

Stockdale's principles were tested when he was asked to write a letter to the US government denouncing the war effort and all those involved. He refused time and again until, after his captors exhausted most of their torture methods, he was subjected to the rope trick. The captors would tie the POW's wrists together behind his back until all circulation was cut off. They would then pull on the ends of the rope, lifting higher and higher. This would bend him forward, and they would start to pull the POW's arms out of their sockets—causing enormous pain and feelings of claustrophobia.

Admiral Stockdale realized that he needed to expand the scope of the Code of Conduct for his fellow POWs or they wouldn't survive. He told the other POWs to resist to the utmost of their capabilities, but not to the point of death. He encouraged them instead to deceive, to give false information—to do anything that might frustrate the interrogators. Collectively, the new vision, the new focus, was for all to "return home with honor." This became a mantra that boiled down the six articles into a powerful capsule, and it gave Stockdale and his fellow POWs the focus they needed in unimaginably vile circumstances.

If POWs are able to focus on an important vision in such an intense, life-threatening situation, you should be able to do it too—no matter how intimidating your leadership role seems.

We Can Only Do Three!

Just as Admiral Stockdale knew about focus in the sphere of war, Steve Jobs knew how crucial focus is in the professional world, as Walter Isaacson showed so vividly in his bestselling biography of the Apple leader. Writing about his book in *Harvard Business Review*, Isaacson says that many commentators sprang up around the book's release, hoping to derive management lessons from Jobs's life; some of these analyses were on target, while others weren't. Among the real keys to Jobs's success, Isaacson points out, the very first is focus. "Focus was ingrained in Jobs's personality and had been honed by his Zen training," Isaacson writes. "He relentlessly filtered out what he considered distractions." [40]

Think about it: One of the reasons Apple is such a great company is that it puts out beautiful, easy-to-use products. But another reason Apple is so successful is that everything the company makes can fit on one giant table. Ever visited an Apple store? If you took one of each of its products—iPad, iPod, iPhone, iMac, etc.— you would be able to carry the entire selection out of the store in one big shopping bag.

When Steve Jobs made his return to Apple in 1997, the company was nearly bankrupt—it had sixty days of cash left—and was producing dozens of different types of products and peripherals. He shut down 1,040 projects and focused on four major categories: Consumer, Pro, Desktop, and Portable. Then he assembled his top one hundred teammates and brainstormed products, ideas, and what Apple should be doing next. They whittled the list down to a top ten, and then Jobs slashed that list further. He was famous (or infamous) for saying, "We can only do three!"

Three products—that was it. It probably sounded crazy at first, but few today can deny that Apple's leadership, no-holds-barred approach brought the company amazing success.

This is a great example of how a clear vision leads to focus. If you're laser-focused on three things, there's a pretty good chance that you are going to be successful at those three things, whatever they might be.

Paint the Full Picture

If you want your vision to be effective, you have to paint a full, vivid picture of the desired end state. The more realistic and vibrant your conception of where you want to be, the more it will keep your team—and you—on track toward the goal.

My friend Doc Hendley was in the bartending business when he founded Wine to Water, a 501(c)(3) aid organization, in 2004. Doc's vision was very clear: He wanted to provide clean water to people who needed it around the world. The original concept was to put on benefit events, such as wine tastings, and use all the money raised to support water projects around the world. The first fundraiser was a great success. With its success, followed by other winning efforts, came a confidence that Wine to Water would continue to grow as an organization. As a result, wine tastings became just one of many ways that Wine to Water raises awareness and support for the global water crisis.

Doc's vision of providing clean water where it's needed has helped him be the catalyst for a team that does great things. And one of the reasons he's been so successful is that he's really painted a vivid, emotional image of success. According to Doc, even when he was most challenged—in a ragtag camp in the middle of Darfur, in an area that the United Nations had declared a "no-go zone"—he reflected back on a time when he watched children experience clean water in their hometown for the first time. No more hiking for hours to the nearest water source! The kids soon realized they had much more free time—time to actually play instead of hike for water.

Time and again Doc has revisited this memory of children playing freely, to remind himself of his vision—why he was in that inhospitable, worn-out land, even when all he wanted to do was get out of Darfur and go home. The vision of the joy of children who've been granted a reprieve from the water crisis is so powerful that it inspires him to keep going. Today, his team has provided clean water to many countries, including Sudan, India, Cambodia, Uganda, Ethiopia, and Haiti. By the end of 2011, they reached their hundred-thousandth person. By 2015, they plan to have reached their millionth.

Take a cue from Doc and center your vision on what success looks, sounds, and feels like. Bring it to life. Let people experience what it's going to be like when they work toward and arrive at the goal, and they'll be even more committed and driven.

Remember, uncertainty breeds anxiety. Once you've clarified the win by painting a picture of it, you've removed the uncertainty and thus reduced the anxiety. A team can't function as a team unless there is a goal, a point at which you can claim success—a defined win. And yet you can be part of an organization for years and years and never know exactly what the win looks like. Don't let that happen on your team!

Realize That Your Vision Doesn't Have to Be Perfect

So you're the catalyst—the one with sole responsibility for creating a vision that lights your people up; but what if you aren't sure the vision you have in mind is the perfect one? What if you aren't sure how to make that vision a reality? It doesn't matter. Setting *any* vision is going to be far more valuable than leaving it nebulous. You don't have to get into the details of how that success is going to come. You just have to set a vision that catalyzes your team into action.

Remember the story of the men who got out of the Alps using a map of the Pyrenees? Of this story, Karl Weick, author of *Sensemaking in Organizations,* once said, "When I described the incident of using a map of the Pyrenees to find a way out of the Alps to Bob Engel, the executive vice president and treasurer of Morgan Guaranty, he said, 'Now, that story would have been really neat if the leader out with the lost troops had known it was the wrong map and still been able to lead them back.'"[41] Engel's twist to the story pinpoints the basic situation that most leaders face: They know the general objective (whether it's getting out of the mountains alive or keeping a division profitable), but they may not be sure where to go next. The leader in Engel's hypothetical situation acknowledges that the map isn't the right one, but he also knows that it nevertheless gives his people something to aim for.

The soldiers were able to produce a good outcome from a bad map because they had a vision (to get back to camp): an image of where they were and where they were going. Plus, they took action: They kept moving, noticing cues, and updating their sense of where they were. As a result, an imperfect map proved to be good enough. The same goes for your vision. The important thing is that you put it out there and let it catalyze people into action. You can always adapt and adjust along the way.

Use the Vision to Create Purpose

A 2013 survey from professional services powerhouse Deloitte, *Culture of Purpose: A Business Imperative*, indicates that there is a link between a sense of purpose among employees and long-term organizational success.[42] In fact, 91 percent of all respondents who said their company has a strong sense of purpose also cited its history of strong financial performance. However, 68 percent of employees and 66 percent of executives believe businesses neither do enough to create a sense of purpose nor deliver meaningful impact.

When employees lack clarity on your organization's mission, they don't see themselves as part of the solution. They start to withdraw and disengage from your team and from the company. This can be devastating to both the employee and your organization. Your job as a fearless leader is to clarify that mission and then bridge the gap from the possible to the impossible—to help your team go beyond what they currently think is possible and to believe they can do the impossible. Having a fully developed, fully articulated vision will give your team a sense of purpose. It will allow them to overcome the extraordinary obstacles they face and break through the barriers that keep them from achieving their personal and professional dreams.

Ask yourself and your team, "What is the problem we are here to solve? What are our goals?" Drill down on this, and it will energize your team. You can also turn it around this way: "What won't happen if we *don't* do _____?" These simple questions give the team a shared reason to exist—a clear, compelling purpose that is important to each of the

HAVING A FULLY DEVELOPED, FULLY ARTICULATED VISION WILL GIVE YOUR TEAM A SENSE OF PURPOSE.

individual team members. A sense of purpose creates both context and a feeling of urgency. It is the single most important factor in a team's success.

Go Big, Be Bold

Oftentimes we hear people talking about Big Hairy Audacious Goals (BHAGs)—the truly aspirational goals leaders say they want to achieve. The problem is, these objectives are not even remotely achievable or believable. And when the gap between the goal and your current situation is too big, it can actually be a demotivating factor instead of a motivating and inspiring target for your organization.

Fearless leadership takes guts, and history shows us this is not easy. So what should you do? Stop setting big goals? Won't that lead to average results and mediocrity? Not necessarily. The key is to set a big goal with a very clear, step-by-step path for your team to achieve that vision. Gaining little wins along the way will increase confidence and keep your team engaged. High-performing teams and peak performers are able to see value in the small wins en route to the big win. They are able to break BHAGs down into a series of smaller goals that mark the path to the ultimate victory.

Craft a Memorable Vision Statement

As we've discussed, painting a picture (however imperfect) that offers purpose—an important goal that can be reached step by step—is critical. Your job as a fearless leader is to communicate your vision so clearly that everyone on your team can internalize it and execute according to your organizational values. One way to do this is to boil your vision down into a *vision statement:* a tagline that reminds people of that full picture of success you're all working toward. Crafting that vision is tough work and requires constant dialogue, repetition, and reinforcement.

Keeping your vision out front is one of the most valuable things you can do to create a high-performing team, and the vision statement is a great way to do that. When it's reinforced on a regular basis, the vision starts to get into your subconscious so that without even thinking about it, you are pulled toward that vision; it determines your actions—the steps that you will take to get there. The vision statement—the boiled-down version of that vivid picture you painted—will start to propel your team forward.

In order to make the vision statement accessible at all times, it needs to be short, simple, memorable, and repeatable. This can be painstaking work; oftentimes the simpler the statement is, the more time somebody has actually spent crafting it. But if you want your vision to stick, it's really important to take the time to do this right.

The more people you need to get behind you, and the more complicated the steps ahead of you, the simpler and more memorable your vision statement needs to be. Make it succinct and transferable. It should communicate to people instantly, without explanation. The best people aren't looking to work for a company with a long, verbose, or grandiose vision statement! They want to give their time and energy to an organization with a straightforward purpose, to a team that is on a mission.

Want to know what *doesn't* work? Vision statements that are saddled with boring, corporate-speak gobbledygook. Let me share an example. I'll preface this by saying that I love Volvo's super-safe vehicles and its great record of superior engineering. But here is the company's vision statement: "By creating value for our customers, we create value for our shareholders. We use our expertise to create transport-related products and services of superior quality, safety, and environmental care for demanding customers in selected segments. We work with energy, passion, and respect for the individual." What the heck does that even mean? That wouldn't fire me up to get out of bed on a frosty morning in Sweden! "Market leading," "value for shareholders," "best experience in the markets we serve"—ugh. It's not very convincing to the customer—there's too much jargon, and it's neither aspirational nor inspirational.

Now let's look at BMW: "The Ultimate Driving Machine." Yeah, buddy, that's something I can get behind!

How about Google: "Organize the world's information and make it universally accessible and useful." That's pretty clear-cut.

Think Nike: "Just do it."

Barack Obama: "Change." Do you remember Hilary Clinton's vision? Mitt Romney's? Obama's was the most memorable. He didn't have to fill in all the details, but everyone knew what his vision was. Politics aside, both those who liked him and even those who didn't knew that he stood for change.

The F-14 Tomcat community had the legendary "Anytime Baby!" slogan. It was embroidered in bold letters on a patch next to a spunky, gun-slinging tomcat mascot and prominently displayed by F-14 pilots.

The phrase was originally thrown out as a challenge to the US Air Force's F-15 Eagle to go one-on-one against the F-14 in a dogfight. The F-14 prevailed. "Anytime Baby!" lived on as a powerful, unifying statement of what F-14 pilots and their aircraft were capable of.

Don't force-feed your team muddled goals, philosophies, strategies, and corporate-speak. Complicated vision statements don't work. Instead make it short and sweet. Then write it down. Put it where everyone can see it. Read it often. Repeat it often. Repetition, repetition, repetition. As personal success expert Napoleon Hill once said, "Any idea, plan, or purpose may be placed in the mind through repetition of thought."

Make It Personal

Great squadron commanding officers, great leaders, and great managers will all share with you the importance of not only knowing yourself, but also knowing your people. As you cast your vision, knowing your people and what matters *to them* is just as important as understanding your mission. Your team members' goals, strengths, and weaknesses will help you understand their ability to accomplish your mission, to achieve your vision.

One of the most humble, talented, and confident leaders whom I've had the good fortune to work with over the past few years is Bill McCarthy, vice president of sales at Cisco. Bill is one of the most effective, self-aware leaders I've ever met. He has the ability to clearly articulate his vision and goals for his teams, goals that motivate them to generate tremendous results.

Bill is so respected in the IT world because he just gets it. He has the secret sauce of courage, tenacity, and integrity—the mojo. What makes Bill so impressive is his ability to turn a highly sophisticated company vision into something personal for each and every person on his team. He takes the lofty, aspirational goals of the organization and makes them personal.

It's no different from the importance of ensuring that every member of your fighter squadron understands where you want the squadron to go. Simply telling your team your goals for the future is not good enough, and Bill understands this. He goes to extraordinary lengths to not only define the vision—where he wants the team to go—but also consistently share it with them over and over and over. In every forum possible—large meetings, phone calls, personal visits—Bill shares the vision, but then he takes it a step further: He listens to the feedback from his teammates. What are their goals? What are their dreams? He understands that in today's noisy working environment, too many people tend to forget what their leaders shared with them yesterday unless it actually matters to them—unless they can internalize the vision.

He is also authentic; he doesn't pretend to have all the answers, and he is more than willing to ask questions. He really listens—for the sake of understanding, not just to think about what his next response is going to be. Congruency, consistency of message, involving his team, and listening—these are Bill's hallmarks, and they earn the understanding, engagement, and respect of others—both those above him and those who work for him.

Bill shared with me that he is "strategically focused, but tactically minded about getting things done." Here's how he explains his approach:

I try to bring the personal, the tactical, all the way through the strategy to the individual so each person sees how it applies to him or her. You have to *own* the vision and be able to *explain* the vision in a way that your people care and are able not only to see how it applies to them, but also trust you to *take them with you.* And then you *live* that vision with them. You communicate that vision hundreds and hundreds of times.

How do you reinforce that vision? Bill illustrates it like this:

> You can almost think of it like a campaign. That's how much work it will take—like you're running for office as you establish that vision, that platform. You remind people, "Here's what we are working on, here is what we are trying to accomplish," and you use the common language, the terminology to get people aligned to that vision. You then lay out a strategy that engages your team and gets the personal interest of the people you are talking to, and you share with them what the future could look like. This takes time, energy, and attention. You cannot shortchange this process. Eventually your "brand" precedes everything else: who you are within the organization, what matters to you, what you value. The team that you are leading should already know quite a bit about you; they should know what they are going to get. Again, this requires consistency in your behavior and your message. This establishes trust.[43]

This takes a high level of personal investment. Bill clearly reflects and embodies the cultural values that he wants to be known for: integrity, honesty, authenticity, and excellence. But he also has the expectation that his team should emulate those values. So when he establishes the vision and sets those aspirational goals, those big bets, Bill is able to get his people to embrace the vision. They know what matters most, what is valued. The goals and expectations are clear; he makes sure they have all the resources they need; and they start executing.

A great vision and the right strategy, followed by fantastic execution by the right team members, are what drive the results on Bill's team. He has developed a very specific, very personal path to a high-performing culture within his team—and it starts with his vision:

> # A GREAT VISION AND THE RIGHT STRATEGY, FOLLOWED BY FANTASTIC EXECUTION BY THE RIGHT TEAM MEMBERS, ARE WHAT DRIVE THE RESULTS.

- They know what to expect from him as a leader *(consistency)*.
- They know the path ahead *(alignment, purpose)*.
- They know the right people are onboard *(team building)*.
- They are convinced he will help them achieve their goals *(trust)*.
- They know he will be ruthlessly, but politely, honest *(candor, transparency)*.
- They know he is prepared, informed, and willing to ask questions *(excellence, continuous improvement)*.
- They know what behaviors are expected *(culture)*.
- They know he will be working just as hard if not harder than they are to achieve this vision *(motivation)*.
- They know that he is serious about excellence in execution, but also that he wants to have fun *(authenticity)*.

All this is the epitome of a fearless leader, and it makes Bill a pleasure to work with.

Creating Alignment from Janitor to CEO

Everybody at every level in our organization on an aircraft carrier, whether a petty officer working on the flight deck or a seaman working ten levels down in the laundry room, knows how his or her individual performance impacts the organization's success. The same should be true in your world. You need your staff—your teammates—to commit to the vision, not just meekly agree to go along and get along. We want wholehearted embracing of the plan; we want synergy. And for that to happen, the environment needs to allow and encourage discussion so people can embrace the move-forward plan, knowing that it is rooted in the collective wisdom of the entire group.

While presenting at an operational excellence workshop in Milan, Italy, with attendees from all around Europe, representing many different types of organizations, I was sharing why so many aggressive process-improvement programs falter and how to prevent this from happening—essentially tying together the powerful disciplines of Lean Six Sigma with a high-performing team. One of the areas I touched on was the importance of all hands—all of your team members—understanding clearly how their performance specifically ties to the success of the organization.

During the question-and-answer section, the CEO of a premier, high-end porcelain fixtures company remained skeptical about the value in everyone having to understand the vision. He challenged my position: "Why should the janitor have to understand the vision of our company? That's not relevant to his performance. How does he impact our bottom line?"

I asked him about some of his company's specific challenges. His response was quality control. I asked, "What types of quality control issues are you having?"

"Too many cracked fixtures."

I asked, "Why do you think that is?"

He said, "We are getting random dust and particulates in our mixtures, and some of the fixtures are cracking after installation in our customers' projects."

Hmm. Interesting, I thought. "And why are you getting this dust in your mixtures?"

He replied, "We think it is because the janitors aren't doing a good job at night keeping the manufacturing floors clean."

"So don't you think it would be a good idea to loop the janitors in on your vision, so they can see why what they do *matters*?"

Cue crickets chirping.

Finally he replied, "Yes. Yes, I do."

Onboard the aircraft carrier, working in the ship's laundry is not one of the most coveted jobs. During an average six-month deployment, the ship's laundry processes more than 150,000 pounds of laundry per week. As you can imagine, five thousand people working daily with cable grease, paints, jet fuel, hydraulic liquids, and unpronounceable chemicals makes for dirty work. Add to that the fact that the laundry rooms are deep in the bowels of the ship, meaning they can tip the thermostat at 110 degrees sometimes. It's just crappy duty.

Trying to keep this team of sailors motivated and engaged while they process and clean thousands of nasty garments, bedding, and linens daily can be a challenge, as you can imagine. But it is critical to the health and welfare of all those aboard that the laundry is clean and sanitized. Otherwise, five thousand crewmembers could become sick in an instant. It is really important work that, if not done well, can have serious consequences. Norovirus, anyone? And we don't have the luxury of just pulling into port and sanitizing the ship; this isn't a Carnival cruise.

So, laundry duty is not glamorous, but it is critical to the success of the entire team. When the team members clearly understand their role, they can go about their duty with much more pride and ownership, knowing that they matter; they make a difference. They help make the vision a success.

Fearless leaders realize that every team member needs to understand how what he or she does contributes to the overall success of the organization. Every individual contributor, plant worker, or retail clerk in your organization needs to understand what *value* he or she brings to the team and how it can help the team achieve success.

Too often, we depend on a simple job description—medical salesperson, administrative support—to motivate our team members. That just doesn't work. If your teammates are not rallying around your mission, it's probably because either your vision or your vision statement is not clear. Your people need more than a list of duties to perform; they need your help in envisioning their place in the overall scheme of things. People want to belong to something bigger than them. They want to be on your team—so figure out a way to get them onboard, to express your vision so that other people get it. Help your team go farther and faster!

After you've shared your vision, one of the most difficult leadership challenges you will face will be to create alignment between your vision and goals and those of the people you lead.

Remember the legendary story about JFK visiting NASA headquarters? Purportedly the president stopped to talk to a man with a mop, asking, "And what do you do?" To which the janitor replied, "I'm helping to put a man on the moon, sir." That's how it has to be!

When your teammates know their part in the company story—how they are helping create success—you'll know you have a clear vision that has been well communicated throughout your organization. Your vision needs to become *their* vision.

Fearless leaders are able to make their goals the team's goals. They know how to make the goal relevant to the people they lead. It is impossible to lead any great team or organization of any size or kind without getting your people aligned, fired up, and intensely focused on the mission.

Without alignment you are dead in the water; your ship will go nowhere. You can have the best division, the best team members, or the best idea in the world, but you won't make it happen if you can't get the people onboard to all start rowing in the same direction. If you can't get alignment, your ship is sunk.

Once you've defined the vision, you must be very clear about what it is you want your team to accomplish. There will be those who want to know, "What's in it for me?" So, you have to drive the change. Orient people to a compelling end state; create buy-in, and show the value in it for them *personally*.

A great visual example of team alignment is the US Navy Blue Angels. Traveling wingtip-to-wingtip at more than 400 miles per hour, the Blue Angels set the standard for shared alignment and shared goals.

We need to have an end state that everyone can align toward. Think about the Blue Angels: With intense focus, purpose, and discipline, they can master the skies at 400 mph while flying 24 to 36 inches apart! Alignment then allows us to exercise initiative—we know what success should look like. Whether you are the most senior officer on a nuclear-powered aircraft carrier or the most junior seaman on the ship, each person must be empowered, because any given individual may be the one in the right place to prevent a mishap.

What happens if you don't get alignment? What does your team's performance or your end-of-year look like? Lost opportunities. We don't need "perfect" alignment; striving for that misplaced ideal can inhibit innovation and stifle diversity of thought. But if a teammate starts heading off in a wrong direction, that is a coaching opportunity. With clear objectives and good alignment, everyone can do their job. You can now pursue excellence.

*   *   *

With a simple, repeatable, inspiring vision in place and the team aligned around it, your people will be looking forward, not backward. Together, you'll go farther and get there faster, and you'll have what it takes to fly over obstacles. As Twitter founder Jack Dorsey has said, "You can constantly look in your rearview mirror, and you can constantly look around and really not notice the road ahead of you. Or you can focus on what is ahead of you and drive. And drive fast."[44] That speed and that focus are what fearless leaders create when they establish and share their vision.

> ## THAT SPEED AND THAT FOCUS ARE WHAT FEARLESS LEADERS CREATE WHEN THEY ESTABLISH AND SHARE THEIR VISION.

The vision also serves as a foundational piece of your team's culture. Once you have established a vision, it's time to let that defining purpose trickle down to the day-to-day of your team. Your vision sets the tone for the actions of your team: how they collaborate, cooperate, celebrate, and grow, which is the subject of the next chapter. And a great vision followed up with a great strategy translates intention into focused action, which we'll dig into in chapter 6.

Chapter 5

CULTURE

BRINGING PEOPLE TOGETHER IN A HIGH-PERFORMING TEAM

Any time you lose your wingman, you've lost
75 percent of your eyes and fighting strength.
—Lieutenant Colonel Robert Johnson, legendary
World War II US Air Force pilot

My days aboard the aircraft carrier started with this announcement from the Air Boss: "On the flight deck, pilots and crews are manning aircraft for the first launch of the day. Check your helmets on, chin straps buckled, goggles down, sleeves rolled down, and flotation vests securely fastened. Check for loose gear about the deck. All nonessential personnel, clear the flight deck!"

Every morning, with those words, the flight deck of a US aircraft carrier comes to life. Operating in a complex and dangerous workplace unlike any other in the world, the carrier team's work during flight operations looks to the uninitiated like utter chaos. Topside, those critical flight deck personnel are all clumped into groups that each seem to have their own mission. And these people are *young*—on average, 19.5 years old. Teenagers! Top it all off with the fact that they swap out every nine months, and you have what sounds like a recipe for disorder and disaster.

And yet this diverse, thousands-strong team is able to conduct carrier operations seamlessly—launching, recovering, and moving aircraft and people in a safe, efficient, effective, seemingly effortless way. How?

They can do this because they've been unified into a high-performing team—one that works together toward a shared vision . . . trusts absolutely . . . communicates effectively . . . and displays a committed, disciplined, positive attitude. This team is defined by strong working relationships between truly dedicated professionals who operate with a mission-first mentality. Its members know they are part of something bigger than any single individual, and they are motivated to do their part, whether small or big, in helping the team reach its objectives. Every sailor on deck is a specialist; they are all committed to excellence. They are all part of a team focused on success.

Success in any kind of leadership—not just military—requires that the leader build the same kind of cohesiveness and teamwork. Once you've put forth your vision and shown everyone how it relates to their work, you're going to be called upon to lead the team through the day-to-day of working toward that vision, providing hope and encouragement to get through trying times and ensuring that your teammates are performing at their peak capability. In other words, you're going to have to make sure your team is a high-performing team.

You can have the best supply chain or the best widget or the most advanced equipment in the industry, but without the right people on your team working together productively, sustained high performance will be impossible. To succeed, fearless leaders must bring the right people together and ensure that they share common goals, work collaboratively, and encourage a positive spirit.

This won't happen by accident or by hoping; it won't come from good luck or finger crossing. It takes guts, grit, perseverance, and of course, fearlessness. But it's also rewarding work that gets you and your team where you want to go—faster. Witnessing a group of people coming together around a common goal is a beautiful thing, and as a leader, you have the privilege of playing a key part in that process. Harness and bring together the gifts, talents, and passions of your team, and you can go farther and faster with a lot less effort.

Emulate the Carrier Team

By all outward appearances, being a fighter pilot *seems* like the most glamorous position on that aircraft carrier, and it may be. I'm biased. But in reality, we pilots would not be able to do our jobs successfully alone. It takes a team—one that is engaged, that never stops learning and innovating, that can embrace adversity, and that is just as committed to the mission's success as we are. Our teammates' attention to detail in this extraordinarily demanding environment can save our lives.

At the helm of this orchestrated chaos, perched high above the flight deck in the carrier's control tower, is the air officer, affectionately referred to as "the Air Boss" or simply "the Boss." He or she rules the flight deck, supervising and directing all flight deck operations, all aircraft handling, and all movement on the flight and hangar decks. The Air Boss is constantly chatting on the loudspeaker for all flight deck personnel to hear, communicating risks and even asking questions of the folks on the flight deck.

The Air Boss's right-hand man (or woman) is the assistant air officer or "Mini Boss," a wingman to the Air Boss. The Mini Boss provides mutual support to the Air Boss, and they are a close-knit team.

All the sailors on the flight deck are covered in safety gear: a helmet (cranial) fitted with sound attenuators, double hearing protection, goggles, a float coat (life jacket), reflective tape, a long-sleeved flight deck jersey, steel-toed boots with nonslip soles, and fire-retardant gloves. I might not know all their names and faces, but I can quickly identify their roles by the colors of their shirts.

The brown shirts are our plane captains; they monitor our aircraft at start-up, make sure that the airplanes are clean and ready for flight, and service and inspect the aircraft before and after each flight. The purple shirts, or "grapes" (we like to keep things simple), are aviation fuel crews. They fuel up the aircraft.

The red shirts are "ordies"—ordnance personnel—or crash-and-salvage teammates. The ordies handle all the weapons, missiles, and bombs, making sure they are ready to work or disposing of them if necessary.

The top-notch mobile firefighting crash-and-salvage crews look like baked potatoes in all of their aluminum foil–like fire-retardant gear. Don't be fooled; they are fearless—and badass. Those sailors are tough as hell and *will* go headlong into a burning airplane to drag your tail out. (Don't believe me? Google "F-14 Ramp Strike." You'll see what they have to deal with.)

The green shirts work the catapult and arresting gear, do general maintenance, and check the aviation electronics—or "avionics," as we call them. The catapult crew makes sure our aircraft is ready for a safe catapult launch. They communicate with the catapult control officer, passing along aircraft type, gross weight, and side number—critical information to make sure there is enough thrust on the catapult so that we get safely airborne in just under two seconds.

The green shirts are our last line of defense, our last safety check personnel before launch. A moment's inattention—a simple breakdown in teamwork or communication by this bunch—could mean catastrophe.

How so? If they enter an incorrect weight on the weight board— for example, one that is too low or that reflects the wrong aircraft type—this information gets passed along to the personnel who are setting the amount of thrust that will launch us off the front end of the ship. Too much pressure loaded into the catapult shot—a situation called a "hot cat"—can rip out the jet's nose wheel assembly or launching bridle, damaging the aircraft. On the other hand, a too-low weight setting means not enough thrust on the catapult shot and thus not enough launch pressure, so the jet will depart the flight deck well below flying speed. This situation, called a "cold cat," puts the pilot in the "not going flying today" category, and he or she will have to eject. This happened to a friend of mine on a training deployment in the F/A-18 Hornet. He had a cold cat shot at night, and his airplane literally dribbled off the front end of the aircraft carrier. He didn't even have time to eject. It was a tragic loss.

George C. Wilson, author of *Supercarrier,* said, "An aircraft carrier's flight deck is a million accidents waiting to happen." Every flight operations cycle of launching and recovering aircraft is filled with constant activity: engines starting, aircraft taxiing, people running all over, the Air Boss barking orders on the loudspeaker, aircraft launching and recovering, mechanics on top of airplanes doing engine maintenance turns, the constant parking and re-parking of airplanes, the "grapes" running around fueling aircraft—more than one hundred jobs are going on at the same time. The margin for error is slim. Each individual's survival and success on the flight deck hinge on teamwork.

Even though we, as members of the carrier team, operate with extensive standard operating procedures (SOPs) to assess hazards and minimize and manage risk, those procedures alone won't keep you from getting blown overboard, sucked into an intake, or run over by a landing airplane. Everyone on the flight deck must know by heart and quickly recognize all safety signs and signals. Everyone must work together to stay safe, and each teammate plays a role in improving our chances of completing our mission successfully.

Milling among the masses are the white shirts: air wing quality control personnel, squadron plane inspectors, air transfer officers, liquid oxygen crews, medical personnel, and in some cases, landing signal officers. These are the folks who ensure the safety of the carrier's personnel and equipment every step of the way.

Then there are the yellow shirts—aircraft handling officers, catapult and arresting gear officers, and plane directors. To be successful at my job, I must have an extremely close working relationship with these yellow shirts, because they give me very specific directions on when and where to taxi my airplane. The safety margins are razor thin, often requiring me to taxi through super-tight spots between airplanes, where one miscalculation could cause millions of dollars in damage. A slow response to one of their directives could mean death—mine or someone else's. As soon as I release the brake pedals on my $50 million fighter, I watch the yellow shirts' signals intently. When one of them puts his arms up in a high X, I stop immediately. When he signals to step on just one brake, I do it unquestioningly.

In order to safely navigate around other multimillion-dollar aircraft without blowing anyone overboard, my head must constantly be on a swivel. Tailpipe courtesy—knowing which direction my thousands of pounds of thrust is pointed—is critical. The blast of air that one extra millimeter of throttle delivers as I work to position my 30-plus-ton fighting machine is strong enough to send several people over the side of the aircraft carrier. It's a 60-foot drop, akin to hitting a concrete wall, and it's usually a fifty-fifty chance as to whether we will actually be able to spot a man overboard. Obviously, the chances of a recovery are even lower at night.

Imagine working on that deck twelve to fourteen hours a day, seven days a week, 365 days a year in the Gulf of Iran—in temperatures that are quite possibly hotter than hell. It's a hostile environment. It's sensory overload, and it is exhausting.

Now imagine attempting to reposition a 50,000-pound aircraft around the deck under those conditions *and* in the dark. Sometimes— maybe once a year—we lose aircraft over the side. But the fact that we lose the occasional aircraft is hardly amazing; the amazing thing is that any aircraft are *left* at the end of each deployment! That such losses happen so rarely is a testament to the skill, ability, and courage of our fighting men and women on those flight decks.

Perhaps most impressive of all is the fact that this ecosystem is replicable. It is filled with teammates who are committed to excellence and are learning constantly from dedicated, invested mentors. The learning curve is so quick that we can operate effectively even with an extraordinary turnover rate. The military is able to perform its mission successfully while it molds people from vastly different backgrounds into one unified, task-oriented, high-performance team.

Teamwork. Trust. Mutual support. Communication. Not just buzzwords, but a way of life. Each is behind a host of critical performance and survival skills. And we haven't even launched off the front end of the ship yet.

On the carrier, it doesn't matter what color shirt you wear or what department you're in—for successful completion of the mission, it's all about teamwork. This mentality of cooperation and selflessness is crucial in a high-performing team. Building a successful team is a challenge; getting the right talent onboard, with the right people in the right jobs, is critical.

TEAMWORK. TRUST. MUTUAL SUPPORT. COMMUNICATION. NOT JUST BUZZWORDS, BUT A WAY OF LIFE.

Teamwork has a dramatic effect on the effectiveness and safety of military operations, but it's just as true for organizational performance. An effective team can help a company achieve amazing results. A team that is not working, however, can cause unnecessary disruption, failed delivery, and strategic collapse.

Let's now take a closer look at how you can bring your team together—whether it's large or small, diverse or homogenous, highly skilled or doing grunt work—and get your people moving in tandem toward their objective.

We Survive Solo, but Win Together

The first thing your team needs to understand is this: Especially in fast-paced, high-risk environments, everyone needs a wingman, and solid teamwork is critical for developing world-class results. This was true in my world of fighter aviation, and it's just as true in your world of business. Even though you may be the one in command of your "jet," you usually have a wingman—someone who assists in the day-to-day of your office . . . a squadron of colleagues who take care of and maintain your jet, making sure it is airworthy . . . a team that safely launches and recovers you on each business venture. Someone who "has your back."

If your team is going to avoid errors, accomplish its mission, and rise above the competition, close coordination and collaboration are required. Everyone has to understand their mission objective; they have to trust that someone has got their back, while at the same time making sure they have the next guy's back. You, as a fearless leader, will hold them accountable—not through micromanaging, but by illustrating as often as you can the power of supporting one another.

In my time on the carrier, I had many wingmen, and not just the literal, airborne kind. Clearly those were important. Having a competent, capable wingman flying alongside me could increase my chances not just of winning the engagement, but of survival. I also had plenty of wingmen on the ground, including the sailors in red, brown, purple, green, white, and yellow who allowed me to accomplish my mission objective.

Failing to realize that everyone within the team relies on everyone else will undermine any high-performing team. *Top Gun*–style mavericks will do your team no good—even if you, the leader, are the maverick. As a leader, you must actually model dutiful, well-trained (not maverick) behavior. You have to show people how important wingmen are and how each individual can be a good wingman to his or her teammates. Len "Loni" Anderson IV, a US Navy Blue Angel solo pilot, agrees with the importance of this dynamic. As he explained to me, "To continually sustain the success of any team, whether business or military, pride in being the best wingman possible lifts the overall effort to previously unreachable levels. As a wingman for the Blue

THERE IS NO MAGIC TO IT—JUST DO THE WORK.

Angels, your job is to make the *team* look perfect. It doesn't matter about the individual, and there is no magic to it—just do the work."

Building your team, developing high-performance wingmen, is tough work. The Blue Angels just make it look easy!

Navy aggressor squadrons are the toughest aviation adversaries in the world. The pilots of these aircraft have to be the best of the best, because their job is to provide the most difficult training in the world. They are there to mimic and replicate the capabilities of our enemies, from both a tactical and a mechanical standpoint. Putting us through our paces in peacetime increases our chances of survival during actual combat.

Oftentimes these flights take place on what we called the Tactical Aircrew Combat Training System (TACTS) range. Each airplane is armed with a large pod about the size of a missile, which allows the TACTS to gather and record a bunch of data from each aircraft and its weapons systems while flying on the range. The pod tracks and displays all this information on large screens about the size of an IMAX theater. This information is watched in real time for instantaneous feedback and training, and is also used for detailed debriefing.

Screaming low across the California and Arizona desert at speeds illegal in other parts of the country, we would often play a game of cat-and-mouse with these adversaries. Trying to sneak undetected through a working area while hugging the mountainous terrain would be a success—and not an easy task in an airplane like the Tomcat. The Tomcat was bigger than the smaller airplanes, and their trained, hawk-like eyes could detect even a glint of sunlight off the Tomcat's wings.

More often than not, these intercepts ended up in an engagement: an air-to-air dogfight.

The performance of these squadron fighters was eye watering. They were aggressive, and they were there to win. The air combat maneuver hops were not only exhilarating but physically demanding as well. We were essentially yanking our guts out, trying not to lose sight of the threat while trying to gain the advantage, straining to shoot the other guy down—and to make sure we didn't get shot. Finally when the engagement was done, one of the pilots fighting would call, "Knock it off, knock it off." We would either set up for another go-around or head back to base. It was exhausting—we would regularly crawl out of the plane drenched in sweat—but also some of the most fun flying I ever did.

When you are living life on the razor's edge, you have to know each person's roles and responsibilities. You come to understand that a little bit of backup can go a long way. Part of that relationship is grounded in trust. In every challenge that we faced at AOCS, we were given opportunities to succeed; we were also put in positions where we were practically guaranteed to fail. If one of us failed, all of us failed. What happened if one officer candidate received low test grades, was struggling in the swim events, or kept dropping back during runs? The rest of the class would be punished. From the outside looking in, this may seem like an odd methodology or even pure madness. But it is a stark lesson in how the mistakes of one person can affect the entire group—and how failing to look out for the soldier to your left or to your right can hinder your team's success. In combat, everybody may pay the price for one person's mistake.

In the business world as in the military, you want people to feel their interdependency every day when they show up for work—to feel that having one another's back isn't some kind of obligation or burden but instead is a positive, gratifying path to high performance. If you get it right, your approach and your people's will boil down to this: *What can I do? How can I serve you? How can we go farther faster together on this project?*

So, what can you do to remind your team members how interdependent they are?

Well, you might take a lesson from Phil Martens, CEO of Novelis, an Atlanta-based aluminum producer. Phil gets the unity thing. Early in his tenure, he brought his top leadership together in a series of meetings, hoping to show that he wanted to "move from a fragmented, regional company to a globally integrated company." Conflict was rampant among factions of the company, so every choice he made about the meetings was designed to support the theme of teamwork and oneness.

For the first meeting, he chose Switzerland, famed for its neutrality, as the site. And in the second meeting, when the discord continued, he took a more dramatic step, printing T-shirts that read *One Novelis* on the front for every attendee. "On the way out, there are tables with new shirts," Martens told the team. "If you want to come in to the meeting tomorrow, you have to have it on. If not, you can go find something else."[45] The team's problems weren't solved in one fell swoop, but Martens had made a bold and necessary statement: If we're going to win, we're going to win together.

On the aircraft carrier, we worked as one team divided into smaller, highly specialized subteams. The same is likely true in your organization. When each division is so specialized, so successful—a world-class performer in what it does—the danger is that these subgroups can become tribal: talking mostly amongst themselves, believing they're better than the next guys, looking out for teammates but not for someone wearing a different shirt color.

But working only within silos is unacceptable in most organizations. The only way to meet all the demands in today's highly competitive environment is through conscious commitment to teamwork, where both individuals and small teams take personal responsibility for their actions.

Provide Mutual Support

In the Navy, *mutual support* is our phrase for teamwork, meaning that we back one another up—period. In business culture today, too often the notion of teamwork means helping others only as long as it's easy and convenient to do so. In the heat of battle—and amid the everyday chaos of budgets, critical appointments, and meetings running late—it's easy to lose sight of the big picture. This is when we need our wingman to provide good mutual support.

> THE ONLY WAY TO MEET ALL THE DEMANDS IN TODAY'S HIGHLY COMPETITIVE ENVIRONMENT IS THROUGH CONSCIOUS COMMITMENT TO TEAMWORK, WHERE BOTH INDIVIDUALS AND SMALL TEAMS TAKE PERSONAL RESPONSIBILITY FOR THEIR ACTIONS.

The movie *Top Gun* made this phrase famous: "Never, never leave your wingman." But it has truly been a fighter pilot creed for ages. Mission comes first—and that means supporting your teammate, not seeking personal glory. One of the first things you learn as a fighter pilot is your role as a teammate—how to be a good wingman. And your very first contract with your team is to always be in position:

perfect line abreast, tactical formation. Not too high, not too low, not too far ahead, or too far back. The main attributes of a great wingman are great eyes and the ability to hang with the lead *no matter what*. Being a great wingman requires tenacious flying to maintain formation position regardless of what hijinks the lead is pulling.

A wingman is a precious extra set of eyes. When I'm strapped into my airplane, it is very difficult for me to see anything directly behind the aircraft. It is nearly impossible for pilots to turn around in our ejection seat to check for the threat—which, as Murphy's Law would have it, always shows up shrouded by the sun. Our cockpit field of view is limited, and we have a big blind spot. One person alone cannot see everything. Lined up in what we call a "combat-spread formation," however, we have an unobstructed view of our partner's blind spot, and we can provide visual mutual support. "Check six," we would say—meaning, "Look behind me."

My wingman is the first to warn me about something that I can't see. This second set of eyes can be a lifesaver in a combat environment, and I provide the same mutual support to him. When we're airborne, I know exactly where my teammate is going to be. And I am keenly aware of the advantage of bringing a wingman to the merge. He is a force multiplier; he brings extra firepower and an extra measure of safety. If my wingman sees a missile fired my way and yells, "Break right!" I don't ask questions, I just react. Because I trust him.

Think about how this can work in your organization. Who is your wingman? Who is looking after your blind spots, checking your six? Just as we need supportive teammates in a fighter squadron, we need those same trusting relationships at work and at school. A good wingman stays by your side, increasing your chances of survival and success in a hostile environment.

When that system fails—when ego gets in the way of unity—mission failure is almost assured. In 2004 the US men's Olympic basketball team was filled with legendary superstars. But instead of dominating the field of play, this team suffered an embarrassing collapse on the world stage. Selfish play, lazy performances, terrible shooting, don't-give-a-damn attitudes—they simply didn't play as a team. They seemed too concerned about their own personal glory; each

A GOOD WINGMAN STAYS BY YOUR SIDE, INCREASING YOUR CHANCES OF SURVIVAL AND SUCCESS IN A HOSTILE ENVIRONMENT.

player thought he was better than the rest. And they got clobbered. High-performing teams depend on mutual support and the pursuit of shared goals. This team failed on both accounts.

There's no room for glory seekers on a team that is serious about making the shared vision a reality. Make sure every team member—including you—knows where they need to focus their efforts in order to support your company's mission objectives or future picture. In fast-paced, dynamic, sometimes hostile environments, coordination and cooperation among your teammates will help you to accomplish your goals.

The same steadfast interdependence and synergy demonstrated by wingmen in combat is necessary to transform partnerships with colleagues, coworkers, and friends into collaborative relationships that can help you achieve success. Whether you are a seasoned executive, an entrepreneur, or new to the business world, creating a work environment based on mutual support and trust is crucial to success.

Look for every opportunity to highlight the theme of interdependency to everyone on your team. Start with yourself, by making it clear that you rely on each and every one of your people—and that they can rely on you. Tell them straight up: *None of us can do this alone.* Moment by moment, each member is dependent on each other member to succeed.

No matter how well your team works together, you're likely to face division and disharmony at times. Human nature prevails. It's easy for teams to divide themselves into silos based on their functions and to start thinking their function is just slightly more important than all the others—or to just stop paying attention to what their teammates in other silos are doing. Complacency sets in. It's natural for people to backslide into that default setting—and it's your job to keep that from happening. Model wingman behavior constantly, and demand a culture of mutual support among your teammates.

Encourage Trust and Accountability

In the Navy, we trust our wingmen with our lives—the ultimate trust and accountability. Maybe lives won't be on the line in your day-to-day work, but the performance of your team—and therefore your leadership career—will be. So you have to make sure you've got good wingmen. And to get a good wingman, first you must *be* a good wingman.

Those principles of courage, tenacity, and integrity all come into play. To help your team members be true wingmen to one another, you must nurture trust and accountability among them. Your people can say they've got each other's backs all they want, but if they don't feel it in their gut, the exercise is useless. If they don't show up for meetings on time, if their handshake isn't *really* their word, if they aren't pointing out blind spots, if they aren't fighting for success equally as hard as you are—it's just not going to work. Fearless leaders build a culture of trust and accountability. Everyone on the team must have full faith that they can rely on their wingmen.

When people know their role and trust other parties to do their part, you have a high-performing team. This requires a certain vulnerability from all team members, because true collaboration, teamwork, and partnering can occur only when *both* parties trust each other.

How do you delegate critical tasks to a person you don't trust? How will people trust *you*, their leader, if you don't follow through? Your people should not have to follow up a million times to see if a meeting is still on, or wonder if today is the day you show up on time. In the Navy, we do what we say we're going to do, and that's that.

Follow up and follow through. You'll build the strongest team when trust is a given, and you'll save a ton of time and frustration for everyone on that team. A Gallup study uncovered that among people who have been in a solid, collaborative work partnership, 58 percent of partners "strongly agree" and another 29 percent "agree" that they trust each other. In a poor partnership, less than 3 percent "strongly agree" they trust each other, while 50 percent "strongly disagree." Clearly trust is key element of partnership. For examples of a low-performing team, we need look only to Enron, WorldCom, Circuit City . . . and the list goes on.

When trust and accountability are part of your team's culture, the benefits extend beyond the teamwork angle. The trust should extend all the way up to you, the leader—and it should go in both directions. Show your people not only that can they trust you, but that you trust them to do what's best in support of the team's vision—that you have faith in them. This frees you up from pointless micromanaging and gives employees the freedom to carry out their work in the way they think is best. You'll get results through your people as they repay your trust with dedication and hard work. As J. Keith Murnighan, professor at Northwestern University's Kellogg School of Management and author of *Do Nothing! How to Stop Overmanaging and Become a Great Leader*, writes, "People thrive on trust. As every professional I've ever asked has said, when a leader trusts them more than they expected, they step up to show the leader that they were worthy of her trust."[46] Only by encouraging a culture of trust can you become a truly fearless leader.

Although there are defined leadership roles in any organization— after all, someone needs to be "in charge"—a wingman can be someone on any rung of the organizational ladder. The roles of leader and follower can flow back and forth as the environment changes. In the twentieth century, we had this idea of following a Great Leader over the hill, but that vision wasn't particularly helpful in facilitating people working together effectively. Most people today are not just interested in following; they are interested in stepping up and leading, making an impact. With the guidance of the right leader, that adds up to a team where everyone feels like a contributor, where everyone works together harmoniously.

The aviation industry, for example, is actively managing the cockpit culture and trying to eliminate the days where the captain was king and everyone else was there to serve. If you dared to question the captain's authority, your career was over. Asian aviation cultures in particular continue to struggle with this concept. Complete deference to a senior person, even in the face of pure idiocy or obviously poor choices, looks to be a contributing factor in the 2013 Asiana Airlines mishap that killed three and injured scores of others in San Francisco.

Whether you are trying to have a tough business conversation, or attempting to communicate even when you don't have all the answers, it takes guts to step forward and lead—especially when you don't have the "right" title. A true leader, however, takes on the role of wingman no matter his or her job description.

Inspire a Winning Attitude

A great attitude is like the afterburner for your team—it gives that extra boost that gets you off the ground. Positivity is uplifting and contagious. It's the oil that keeps the machine of your team running smoothly, ensuring that all the parts work well together.

I'm not talking about an artificial, Pollyanna culture of "Oh, yeah, happy to be here, boss! Happy to be part of the team!" (Insert dimples here.) Nor do you want an Eeyore culture, where the answer to "How are you today?" is a sarcastic "Greaaaaat" accompanied by an eye roll. Clearly a big gap exists between artificial enthusiasm and a sincere winning attitude. But establishing truly positive leadership will give your team a sense of security and will point to a brighter tomorrow.

Where does the positivity come from? You. As a fearless leader, you set the tone for the attitude of the whole team. The dynamic of a leader who is negative, down, or critical becomes a weight around everybody's neck; when you hit adversity, your team will be unable to rise to the challenge. A real winning attitude, on the other hand, establishes standards

> A REAL WINNING ATTITUDE, ON THE OTHER HAND, ESTABLISHES STANDARDS OF EXCELLENCE AND PERSONAL DISCIPLINE.

of excellence and personal discipline. It allows you to connect with people, listen to them, and maintain a positive outlook—even in turbulent times like this. It sounds challenging, and it can be. A positive, winning attitude doesn't guarantee success, but a negative one almost always kills your ability to adapt.

Several years ago I had the opportunity to spend several days doing strategic planning with a multinational Fortune 500 company. A large team of more than two hundred people from around the globe had gathered to chart the company's future. After three straight days—long hours of intense planning and discussion—it was time for the separate teams to brief the entire group on their plans. At the end of the different teams' presentations, the CEO stood up and said, "We can't do this. Get rid of eighty-five percent of everything. It's too lofty. The teams will never accomplish any of this!"

You could hear the enthusiasm getting sucked out of the room. Other than the hotel staff refilling water pitchers, every person in the room was crestfallen. In one fell swoop, the CEO had demoralized his team, given them zero reason to ever think big or go after stretch goals, and broken any trust and confidence they had in him as a leader who had their back.

Do you think these teammates felt empowered, as though they were a valuable part of a *committed* team with one mission and one common goal? Probably not, after that lashing. Do you think they trusted their leader's commitment to them? Definitely not. Did they feel like an effective, collaborative team trusted with decision-making power? No way. If you're going to build a high-performing team, you must adopt an attitude that encourages your teammates to trust you and your vision, to work together, to challenge the status quo, to innovate, and to never settle for good enough. Positive leadership gives your team a sense of security that allows them to seek greater and greater levels of success. Yanking the rug out from underneath their aspirations will reshape your culture quickly—and not for the better.

You're not always going to feel positive, of course, but it's your duty as a fearless leader to cultivate a winning, can-do attitude, regardless of whether you're having a great day or a frustrating one. As Bill McCarthy of Cisco once said, "As a leader, you do not have the privilege to wear your negative emotions on your sleeve." That means when you have a bad day, you don't get the luxury of taking it out on your team. Find a way to remain positive by being forward-looking; think of obstacles as opportunities. Don't be fooled into thinking this is artificial optimism; this is part of the mindset of a fearless leader.

Your job is to be the catalyst, to bring your team together and generate buy-in on your vision. You must move the performance needle and inspire your people to get out of their comfort zones. High-performing team members can sniff out negativity, lack of faith, insecurity, and selfishness in a leader. If you mirror positivity and a can-do spirit, however, soon enough your team will be a direct reflection of your leadership style and values.

I was fortunate to have several great commanding officers in my tenure in the Navy. Commander Mike "Flex" Galpin, one of my first F-14 commanding officers, was always a tornado of positivity and action. Even under the most challenging of circumstances, when our squadron was suffering from not only budget cuts but also a high-visibility fatal mishap of a female aviator, he never asked us to do anything that he was unwilling to do himself. When he had to deliver "other" news—the bad news—he pulled no punches. Flex was a fantastic wingman and was excellent at building relationships and passing on his lessons learned. He was clear on what he stood for and on his expectations of his team. He set the bar high and demanded that we go out there and push the envelope—that we become fearless.

Commander William "Billy" Martin was another fantastic leader. As the Naval Air Station Pensacola air operations officer, he consistently led by example and maintained a positive outlook. He would set our mission objectives and then cut us loose, trusting us to get the job done. Whether it was flying our missions or planning and executing one of the best airshows in the country, the annual Blue Angels Homecoming Air Show, he empowered us by giving us great stretch goals. He also was not afraid to go to the mat for his teammates when necessary, and in the face of resistance; he would fight to acquire the resources that enabled us to get the job done—a truly fearless leader who inspired everyone on his team.

Remember to Have Fun

Work hard, play hard—that was the motto of every squadron I belonged to. It shouldn't come as a big surprise that a group of people who are constantly pushing the edges of the envelope, testing both their aircraft's and their own personal performance and limitations, would tend to go big when the opportunity presented itself. When it came to work, we gave it our all—why would our approach to having fun be any different?

Life onboard an aircraft carrier can be exhausting. There are no set work hours; the ship operates nonstop, twenty-four hours a day, seven days a week. And when we pilots are not flying, we still have to do our day jobs as maintenance officers, educational services officers, training officers, safety officers, operations officers, and administrative officers. Sometimes it seems there aren't enough hours in the day to cover all our responsibilities. Furthermore, fighter pilots stand combat alert watches. An Alert 5, for example, required you, for the duration of the four-hour watch, to be strapped into your jet, with all of the starting equipment hooked up, and actually sitting on the catapult, ready for a speedy launch within five minutes. Always being "on" is energy consuming, so we often find relief in humor and shenanigans.

Fun is an often-overlooked partner to a positive attitude, an unassuming but powerful tool in the fearless leader's pocket. When you break out the humor, you have a double positive effect: (1) You minimize any fear you may be feeling as a leader, and (2) you improve morale and bring your team together.

When a team is having fun, you can be quite certain they're working well together. Enjoying a diversion or getting together socially builds camaraderie and esprit de corps and lets team members get to know each other a little bit better. This solidarity can help when the chips are down, tensions rise, and performance matters.

When I was going through AOCS, my brother and all of his friends were already well established in flight school. Knowing what I was going through, they took time out of their busy schedules to make sure I wasn't ever feeling alone on this journey. Well aware that drill instructors often read aloud our correspondence at mail call (or made us read it aloud), they sent postcards with funny or clever greetings—messages that bragged about how easy the training was, asked which DI was the worst, wondered whether so-and-so still had a sloppy uniform . . . You get the drift. I particularly looked forward to the boxes full of cookies and the letters filled with stuff—sand, pieces of candy, whatever they could shove in an envelope—intended to get the attention of the DIs, who would then lavish extra "attention" on me. Ah, the feeling of inclusion. . . . Thanks, guys.

Even though I spent some additional time face down in a puddle of sweat as a result of these goodie packages, I also appreciated that it provided a diversion from the day-to-day routine hammerings by the drill instructors. Every so often you could see that when something particularly clever or funny was sent, even they struggled to keep a straight face. This helped to relieve some of the tension in what was a constantly stressful situation.

Fearless leaders are not afraid to have fun. When the stakes are high and your team is grinding through something particularly challenging, working so hard at times that it *hurts*, injecting a little bit of fun actually can be a very effective play.

Once we got to our squadrons, the shenanigans, usually harmless, continued. Back in the day, it was customary—even fashionable, dare I say—to wear clever, not-quite-accurate nametags when going on cross-country flights. Tradition encouraged us to swap out our birth name for a nametag with a call sign that was somewhat . . . spicy. Many of these call signs were creative acronyms or deliberate mispronunciations, and not all were very politically correct. This is the pilot version of a twelve-year-old boy's fart jokes.

At times our squadron movie nights in the ready room were the highlight of a very long day. These nightly movies, called "roll 'ems," were an opportunity for everyone to come together and de-stress for just a little while. Generally speaking, the plot, dialogue, or any other standard measure of a "good" movie was not a concern. The best were the ones that became "cruise classics," movies that were shown over and over and over, until every aviator had every line memorized. *The Great Santini, Caddyshack, Fletch,* and *Airplane* were some of our favorites.

When there was a particularly gnarly nighttime recovery

happening, as the carrier pitched and heaved in the swells, you could always count on aviators to gather in the ready room. Someone would fire up the popcorn maker, because it was show time—a combination of entertainment, plus "*Thank God I'm not out there,*" plus a little education as well. Who would get aboard on the first try? Who wouldn't? Who would have their "night in the barrel" (meaning ugly passes and multiple go-arounds)? How would our teammates hold up under those conditions?

Having some fun while doing your job should be part of the deal, or you're not doing it right. Don't take yourself too seriously. Have the confidence to laugh at yourself when you make a mistake. If you're not having fun, you're missing opportunities to bring your team together through common experiences. You're missing out on a big part of leadership and life.

Fun is also one of the best antidotes to fear. In an environment where it can all be taken away from you in a moment—where in one catapult shot you can lose a friend—you realize you can't afford to be serious all the time. When your work environment becomes too stressful and too serious, your teammates can shut down. They'll start dreading coming to work, becoming afraid to make mistakes, and withdrawing from others. Laughter can be the best medicine to truly reduce stress and increase morale. Try to find the humor in everyday situations.

Sometimes you can draw on a spirit of fun to lighten the mood

> **HAVING SOME FUN WHILE DOING YOUR JOB SHOULD BE PART OF THE DEAL, OR YOU'RE NOT DOING IT RIGHT. DON'T TAKE YOURSELF TOO SERIOUSLY.**

when something goes awry. Say a big competitor makes a move that could have a major downside for your company, and you're not quite sure yet how to respond. Rather than calling a somber meeting and indicating that the team might really be in trouble, try reinforcing the positive attitude with some off-the-cuff humor: "We've got 'em right where we want 'em!" In this type of situation, a light-hearted response within the team can't hurt—and perhaps it can help take the pressure off as you get to work on recovery.

I've been fortunate to work with Robert Isaman, president and CEO of fuel products manufacturer Stanadyne. An amazing and extraordinarily successful leader, Bob has shared with me his take on the importance of having fun and high-performing teams:

> Somewhere in the lexicon of top business schools over the past two decades, the idea of having fun while driving the great game of business has gotten lost. If you define *fun* as enjoyment, excitement, pleasure, joy, or entertainment, then you get why this is so important. No one wants to come to work and be miserable . . . nor should they have to be. High-performing teams generally have an excess of Type A personalities—people who like to think and move fast, and who by definition are either motivated by a *love to win* approach or by its antonym, *hate to lose.* Pressures will inevitably build. When they do, it is important to have a "fun" standard work-in-process (SWIP) that diffuses the energy positively. Company barbecues, pizza days, family open houses—these events re-create and reinforce the sense of community on the team that is so important for performance. This is critical for high-performing team longevity.

That means it's also critical for *you* if you're going to be a fearless leader.

Celebrate Success

Remember the enthusiasm you and your friends showed as kids, each and every time you did something well? On the basketball court during small-fry games, for example: Make a basket? That calls for high fives. Steal the ball? More high fives, plus some grins and *Woo hoos!* all around.

At what age do we forget how to celebrate our success? Are we too busy? Do we think it doesn't matter? Do we just move on to the next challenge, the next goal, without remembering to enjoy each achievement? I'm not sure.

What I am sure of is this: More and more, I see companies and leaders who have forgotten to acknowledge successful and driven employees as they achieve their goals. And that is too bad; it's a lost opportunity to improve morale, to show your team that you value them and their contribution.

This means recognizing achievements of individuals and acknowledging when the team has done great work. But you don't have to wait until you hit a milestone. *Attaboys* cost your company nothing. You can thank your employees and your teammates in so many different ways, starting with the totally free "Thank you." You may get tired of saying, "Thank you," but trust me—no one ever gets tired of hearing it. Do you? I don't.

> YOU MAY GET TIRED OF SAYING, "THANK YOU," BUT TRUST ME—NO ONE EVER GETS TIRED OF HEARING IT.

Fearless leaders celebrate success and achievement in small, simple ways, and these gestures go a long way toward maintaining and even improving morale. In the Navy, we didn't have the luxury of giving financial bonuses as a reward or to incentivize better performance. So one of the most powerful motivators was to recognize our shipmates' performance—our sailors, chiefs, and civilian support staff—in public, in front of their peers. Depending on how busy we were, generally we would have all-hands meetings once a month, or once a quarter at a minimum. This was a time to bring together all squadron personnel to recognize publicly the good deeds that our shipmates had accomplished.

Recognizing your successes, it seems, can even lead to more success. A 2010 study of soccer players by Gert-Jan Pepping found that the team that celebrated goals with the most enthusiasm typically won the game.[47] No kidding. Their enthusiastic behavior spreads to other teammates and positively motivates them. So give those high fives and cheer your team's success. (Save the butt slapping for sports teams, please. Otherwise—hello, HR nightmare!) It just might make you more successful.

Taking the time to celebrate your team's success builds confidence and makes it easier to keep pushing to reach those stretch goals. It can generate excitement and momentum within your ranks, motivating everyone on the team to continue to work toward your company's future picture.

Celebrating success doesn't require a formal, scripted occasion, but if those who were part of helping to create that success share their insights, perspectives, and lessons learned, you can set your group up for even more success in the future.

Every November 10, all around the globe, United States Marines both young and old salute the birthday of the Corps. Whether celebrating at a formal Marine Corps Ball or in individual toasts to lost Marines, they recognize the sacrifice and service of those who have gone before and those who continue to serve. It's interesting that they celebrate this day as a birthday, not as an anniversary—in recognition of the Marine Corps as a living, breathing entity. Pretty cool. How many other organizations celebrate their birthday? I think there's a lesson here: There are innumerable ways to celebrate both the team and its members in a meaningful way.

When I was deployed with my squadron over to the Gulf, the weather conditions were just unbearable, for the aviators but even more so for the flight deck personnel, who had to work in conditions that oftentimes reached 140 degrees. It was truly hotter than hell and half of Georgia. I could do nothing about the heat, but I could show my teammates that I cared about them and appreciated the work they were doing. So I would go down to the ship's stores and buy big bags of freeze pops, and hand them out in between launch and recovery cycles to all the yellow shirts who were directing and moving our planes. It was a small gesture, but sometimes that's all it takes to make somebody understand that you respect and value his or her contribution to the team. Gestures like this help build trust within a team, increasing the recognition that you are all in this together.

Celebrate your team's successes so people feel proud about what they do and realize they are part of a high-performance family. Leaders don't do enough of this sort of celebrating; they need to push recognition down to a very local level. When you're a well-rounded, unified team, *attaboys* around the office are a common occurrence.

Acknowledgment of overcoming obstacles is frequent. Discussions about what the team did right in the past and where it's now headed are expected and productive.

Celebrating success is a hallmark of high-performing teams. Challenge yourself to promote this within your organization.

> **CELEBRATING SUCCESS IS A HALLMARK OF HIGH-PERFORMING TEAMS.**

Communicate Like You Care

Communication is the lifeblood of teamwork, and once again it's you, the leader, who sets the tone for the whole team. Part of your job as leader is to clearly define and communicate your organizations strategy—but a fearless leader communicates in a way that *inspires* those on your team to remain fully committed and that shows you really give a damn about them. In the heat of battle, too often we completely shut down and dismiss everything going on but the task at hand. This can have a devastating effect on your team. Communication breakdowns are at the root of many organizational problems. Your teammates need to be informed, but they also need to know you care enough to communicate with them in a timely fashion.

Those leaders who can pair great communication skills with a positive, hopeful outlook are much more likely to have a team that works well together, feels it is capable of reaching its goals, and is willing to invest the time and energy required to turn your strategy into reality. It's your job to communicate in a way that gets people revved up and pulling in the same direction—always. Some people say, "Hope is not a strategy." Really? It had better be a part of your strategy to inspire and provide a hopeful outlook for your team.

But you need to do more than just inspire your people to do a great job. You must show them that you understand and care about them as human beings. As a leader, you'll encounter situations where people under you are going through troubling times, whether it's work-related or something in their personal life. Don't be afraid to sit down and talk to them, to show them you have some emotional intelligence. Take the time to really *listen* to what they are telling you, and respond constructively and thoughtfully. This doesn't mean you have to solve their problems, but it's important for your teammates to feel heard—to feel that they matter.

Taking the time to listen allows you to more clearly understand what barriers to performance your people are encountering as well as what skills they have (or don't have) to overcome these barriers. They may need help with this—but you will never know if you don't take the time to listen.

And listening is not always as easy as it may sound. The lines of communication are broken and ineffective when verbal and nonverbal messages are inconsistent. UCLA psychology professor Albert Mehrabian famously found that sometimes there is a disconnect between what people see and what they hear. His work has led many to conclude that *what we say* accounts for only 7 percent of how people perceive us, *the way we say it* accounts for 38 percent, and *what others see* accounts for 55 percent. The simple math is shocking: More than 90 percent of the impression we leave has nothing to do with what we say, but how we say it! So as fearless leaders, we can't just assume that communication has happened and move on.

Stanford Business magazine validates this position: "Research indicates the pitch, volume, and pace of your voice affect *what people think you said,* about five times as much as the actual words you used."[48] Your ability as a leader to communicate effectively involves more than just barking orders; you also need to connect with your team in a way that earns commitment, trust, and loyalty. The esteem of your people is a privilege—not a right. Take the time to learn who people are outside of work and what is important to them. Listen when they share their interests and their problems. Be honest in maintaining relationships. Investing your time in your people will help generate buy-in when, inevitably, you need to change course and you have to have everyone pulling extra hard to set the new trajectory. Be very conscious and intentional with your path to success, and think about the relationships that you build. The more you connect with people on a personal level, the more influence you will have with them.

FEARLESS LEADERS DON'T STEP AWAY FROM THEIR TEAM MEMBERS WHEN PROBLEMS SURFACE, EVEN THOUGH THAT MIGHT BE THE MORE COMFORTABLE ROUTE.

Fearless leaders don't step away from their team members when problems surface, even though that might be the more comfortable route. They step out of their comfort zone and learn to enjoy communicating with employees even through the rough times. They become enthusiastic students of people, which also requires self-awareness.

Ultimately, communicating well with your people will not only make the team more cohesive; it will turn out to be a boon for you personally. No leader gets anywhere alone. If you forgo building strong relationships and act as if you're a team of one, you're almost guaranteed to end up lonely and disillusioned at the head of a fragmented team.

The demands within the fighter aviation environment are always dynamic and often chaotic. On the carrier there has to be constant communication between the aircrew within the cockpit and the flight deck operators. Clear, effective communication is key, and the Navy has developed in its people the ability to communicate quickly—both verbally and nonverbally, with predetermined signals—within the cockpit, from the cockpit to the flight deck personnel, from flight deck member to flight deck member, and with teammates outside of our environment.

In this hostile environment, conditions are frequently unpredictable and mutual support is necessary for team success. Not many groups are better at comm brevity (clipped communications) than Navy fighter pilots. Every transmission of information is specific, brief, and laser-focused:

"Roger."

"Two's up."

"Check six!"

"Fight's on!"

In a high-stress, task-loaded environment, voice control is just as important as proper terminology. This isn't about sounding cool on the radios; it's about being definitive, positive, and concise. The goal is to share the maximum amount of information while using the minimum number of words. Proper communications are vital for safe and successful operations.

Failure to communicate effectively can have disastrous results. Consider this true story, not the only one of its kind: A young Navy sailor was working the flight deck at night. Needing to cross the flight deck in the few seconds available between aircraft landing, the sailor signaled the arresting gear officer by waving his flashlight vertically. After getting acknowledgement from the arresting gear officer via the waving of a green flashlight vertically, the sailor safely sprinted across the pitch black landing area.

When looking to cross back over, the sailor once again signaled to the arresting gear officer and received the same vertical flashlight wave—only in red. The sailor knew that the vertical waving meant it was okay to cross, but didn't know that the color of the flashlight was a critical piece of information. On this particular ship, green meant "go," while red meant "stand fast."

Confusion in communication signals almost cost this sailor his life. Rules for crossing the landing area are forged in blood, and obeying them is crucial. Upon further investigation it was discovered there wasn't a standardized set of signals for this action—they varied from ship to ship. Recognizing the need for a common understanding amongst all teammates, the Navy made an immediate change in procedure.

Though the consequences may not be life-or-death, confusion causes significant, sometimes unnoticed problems in the business world. Too often we shoot off an email or a text and assume that someone has received our message and clearly understands its intent or direction—but that is not always the case. The modern style of communicating has derailed more relationships than we might be willing to acknowledge. Meetings are missed ("But I sent you a text!"), feelings are hurt ("Didn't you listen to my voicemail?"), and opportunities are lost ("Well, I sent you that email last week regarding

the super-critical blah, blah, blah . . .").
Believe it or not, sometimes technology
fails—or the people using the technology fail by depending on the words used
rather than the verbal or nonverbal cues
behind them. You need to have a backup
plan. Remember: Communication has
not occurred until both sides understand
the message.

COMMUNICATION HAS NOT OCCURRED UNTIL BOTH SIDES UNDERSTAND THE MESSAGE.

Set Your Ego Aside

I've spent a lot of time reflecting on and sharing the lessons that I
learned during my time in the Navy, including the idea that top performers *must* be able to set ego aside and be able to communicate with
their teammates. When you start to feel entitled to respect because
of your position—and when you no longer feel the need to ask for
input from your teammates—the consequences can be catastrophic.
Outside of aviation, nowhere is this more apparent than in the realm
of patient safety in hospitals.

When it comes to safety, carrier aviators have it down to a science.
With zero tolerance for error, we rely on every crewmember, regardless
of rank, to work as a team and maintain safety awareness at all times.
The standards of carrier aviation include simple, rigorous checklists;
a culture that doesn't tolerate safety lapses; sound decision-making
skills; clear communication; and a model that requires collaboration
in order to be successful. In short, the same kind of teamwork needed
to eliminate *preventable*, life-ending mistakes in hospitals.

An average of 200,000 Americans die annually in hospitals from preventable medical mistakes. That is the equivalent of 390 jumbo jets full of people.

Three hundred and ninety jumbo jets.

A lack of basic patient safety measures and a complete breakdown in operating room teamwork has catastrophic consequences. In 2008, it cost my dad his life. Had a culture of patient safety, teamwork, and communication been prevalent in the operating room, I wouldn't be sharing this story. Patient safety and risk management is something that we all should be concerned with. A lapse in patient safety steals our loved ones—390 jumbo jets full of spouses, parents, grandparents, children, and friends each year.

My dad was a former United States Marine Corps aviator and a Delta pilot for thirty-six years. He lived and breathed all the concepts of aviation safety. He was a true professional. Safety was always his number one concern. The average traveler has the casual assumption that he or she will arrive at the destination safely; few people give it a second thought. And yet the safety of my dad's crew and passengers was not a responsibility he took lightly. As a child I would ask him about when things got bad in the airplane, be it weather or mechanical issues. Did he ever worry about getting his passengers home safely? His reply was simple: "As long as we know our procedures cold, continue to fly the airplane, and talk to each other, the two of us up front will be okay—and that means everyone onboard will be okay too. And they love their families as much as I do."

He was one of the most humble men I've ever met.

Today's military and commercial aviation communities use processes that keep them 99.9996 percent accident free. These processes cover skill sets for teamwork, clear communication, discipline, collaboration, standard protocols, self-incident reporting procedures, and decision making. In the aviation industry, the concept of "crew resource management" empowers anyone on the flight deck to challenge a pilot if they see a potentially fatal blunder in the making. Naturally, zero safety errors is the goal.

But a fragile culture persists in the operating room. Egos can get in the way, and surgeons are often treated with complete deference because of their sophisticated skill sets. As a result, nurses and other staff hesitate to speak up—even if they see a problem. These supporting teammates often fear being labeled as "insubordinate" if they a question or disagree with a doctor's path of care. Clearly, this causes a huge divide between quality care and the goal of an optimally functioning, high-performing OR team. Understandably, the atmosphere in an operating room can be tense. It is a high-stress environment with tons of patient turnover. But tolerating a certain number of fatalities as the cost of doing business is simply unacceptable.

Poor communication between hospital support staff nurses and surgeons is the leading cause of avoidable surgical error. Improving communication, collaboration, and teamwork between physicians, nurses, staff, and patients is a critical leadership issue. Fearless leadership is required to change the culture and the systems currently in place in US hospitals. Straightforward techniques that are used routinely in the cockpit—such as preflight briefings (preoperative briefings), checklists, the ability to call a time-out or a "knock it off" when there is a concern, and routine debriefs—could all reduce the error rates and save lives.

Health care is becoming ever more sophisticated. With continual advances in technology and equipment, surgeons and physicians can't know everything. No one can perform perfectly at all times, but we can do a heckuva lot better in our hospitals than we are doing now.

It takes a team to be successful. It requires clear communication, conflict management, and an understanding that everyone's role in the operating room is valuable. Sure, we can toss about terms like *patient outcome, patient experience,* and *workload management,* but at the end of the day, if that team doesn't work together and if egos aren't checked, it means your family member may become one of those people on the three hundred and ninety jumbo jets. He or she may not come home.

Patient safety needn't be a victim to failed teamwork and communication—nor should your family member. Work to manage those teammates with inflated egos—or move them out before they poison your culture.

Build a Deep Bench

As you go about building your culture and unifying your people, you're going to do yourself a huge favor if you start with the right raw material. That means getting great people on the team and ensuring that they're constantly growing and improving.

In the military, we have very little control over whom we work with. But for most leaders in the private sector, this isn't the case; it's likely that you have a lot of say in who makes it onto your team, who stays, and who gets the boot. The talent that you hire and retain defines what will happen in your organization's future and in that of your team. If you hire well—if you build a deep bench and surround yourself with superstars—leading will be much easier.

So, assuming your goal is to build a unified team that works great together and operates at peak performance, what should you look for in employees? Start by looking for people who are themselves fearless—who can work through adversity, who display integrity, and who show leadership ability.

A culture of high performance tends to attract people who are willing to work hard. The Navy makes great efforts to attract large numbers of recruits at the front end of the pipeline. A very rigorous screening process further increases chances of getting the strongest people matched up in the right jobs that capitalize on their strengths. One of the reasons the Navy invests so heavily in the Blue Angels is their success as a recruiting tool for the services. Most people never get the chance to see the pride and professionalism of Navy sailors. Airshows, however, are a great opportunity for the Navy to showcase the best of the best.

Perhaps you won't always get to handpick your teammates or hire from outside the organization. No matter the circumstances, though, great leaders are those who identify skill gaps and fill them quickly and effectively, building cohesive teams that get results.

To build a deep bench of high-performance team players, Boeing invests heavily in leadership development. CEO Jim McNerney teaches at the Boeing Leadership Center in St. Louis. He leads from the front, making sure his team understands how much he values them and letting them know that he will hold them accountable. In his words, "We're going to make sure people know we expect them to live by these attributes, both the performance and values nature of them. We are going to measure performance against them. We're going to tie career and job readiness assessments to demonstrate progress in these areas. And we are going to insist that our leaders be models for the entire company of what the attributes are all about. As our people grow, so will Boeing."[49] Fearless leaders never stop wanting to pursue excellence; they take the time to develop defined metrics and goals for their teammates.

There's a lot you can do with even the least prepared people. Still, keep an eye out for hard, honest workers and natural integrity, which is like having a head start. Get the right people on your team, because when you have superstars in place who are already interested in leading, you're much more likely to get cohesion and collaboration.

Zappos is legendary for making this happen, by picking out superstars and drawing on their talent. When hired by Zappos, you get four-week, deep immersion training in how to talk to the customer and what the company's values are. About a month into training, Zappos will pay you for the time you've been there, and if you wish to quit that day, you'll get a $3,000 bonus and the opportunity to exit gracefully. The idea is to screen out those people who "kinda like it" there but aren't really ready to commit the level of intensity and energy that Zappos demands.

Ten percent of new employees choose to opt out. This is not your run-of-the-mill interview process. To get rid of a bad fit early in the process, and to get the employees Zappos really needs in order to become the organization it wants to be, the company's leaders are willing to spend the money up front. Zappos ends up with trustworthy employees who then become not only very deeply engaged in the culture, but also deeply empowered. Employees are allowed to go beyond the call of duty, with no scripts and no timelines, to meet the needs of the customers. They do everything they can to make Zappos a memorable experience, whether you're an online consumer, a supplier, or a visitor to company headquarters.

Companies like Zappos know that hiring superstars isn't enough. It's also important to keep developing the skills of the people you hire and encouraging them to grow. In early 2014 Amazon implemented a policy designed to enhance workers' skill sets: As part of an overall effort to make Amazon a desirable place to work, the company is now offering to pay up to 95 percent of the tuition for its warehouse workers who want to take additional classes—even if those classes are not directly applicable to their role at Amazon. On the flip side, Amazon offers Pay to Quit, which awards up to $5,000 for dissatisfied employees to simply walk away.[50]

We can't just tell our teammates to work harder, smarter, and faster; they are already pedaling as fast as they can. We need to take it a step further by ensuring that they can adapt and by providing the space and the trust to innovate—that's how the magic happens! Being able to develop collaborative teams that leverage your team's collective brainpower will give you a distinct competitive advantage.

Lead by Walking Around

Fearless leadership is not accomplished by sitting behind a desk or by dictating demands via email. Uniting and guiding a high-performing team requires you to be visible to your people on a daily basis.

While addressing a conference where I was the keynote speaker, the CEO of one of the United States' largest grocery chains, a multibillion-dollar enterprise, shared how he regularly gets out of his office and gets into the stores to see what is really happening. He views email as a tool, but he doesn't use it as an *excuse*—he still gets out and in front of his frontline teammates. He invests in face-to-face relationships because he understands their value: Speaking to your people can be the fastest way to pick up on changes in the marketplace. Five minutes of face-to-face, personal contact will do more than a week's worth of emails.

This is more than just MBWA (Management By Walking Around), made famous by management consultant Tom Peters and others. We need a new acronym: FLBWA (Fearless Leadership By

Walking Around). The practice of stopping by to personally connect with your people doesn't just help you manage them; it helps you be a better leader. It shows them that you value interpersonal engagement, and it will encourage them to connect with their colleagues as well—further building solidarity among the team.

The very idea of personal connection with their employees makes some people shudder. Well, too bad. Effective leaders do not build, lead, or manage a high-performing team without knowing the team members well and understanding the challenges they will encounter. FLBWA is critical to your team's success. In setting the tone through your words and actions, remember: You can't phone it in! Getting to know the members of your team requires that you meet them where the action is. Go into their workspace; see the environment that they deal with, day in and day out. Ask probing questions, but more important, *listen* to their responses.

Building these relationships will allow you to take your team to the next level of performance, especially once it becomes ingrained as part of your culture. Whether you are an individual contributor, a manager, a manager of managers, a vice president, or a CEO, your team needs you to show them the way. Only you can help them become better at what they're doing, and success will find you only when you understand them and foster these relationships. Get to know the professionals who work for you—get out of your office! Push away from the email, get out on the deck, and start talking to your teammates!

Create a Mentoring Program

If you want to lead a high-performing team, mentoring is crucial. You can get the ball rolling by setting your people up to mentor one another. When a newer person is taught unspoken rules and tips for success by a more seasoned counterpart, crucial information is preserved and relationships among your teammates grow stronger.

As one of the first female combat pilots flying F-14s in the Navy on and off aircraft carriers, I can definitely speak from experience on the need for mentors—particularly those who can relate to you on a personal level. While I was flying, there were very few other women accessible, either as peers or in senior leadership positions. Being one of such a small group, I found that leading can be a daunting task at times—though it can also be exhilarating and one of the most rewarding things you can do. But sometimes it is also very isolating.

Hanging in my closet is a pair of $150 custom pants made by the legendary Sam's Tailor in Hong Kong. These are not your ordinary pants, but pleated, wool-polyester blend, white pants. They haven't been worn since 1995, but I keep them as a constant reminder of why mentoring matters.

Allow me to explain: Picture yourself on a harbor ferry in the rough waters of Kowloon Bay in Hong Kong. It's after midnight, and as a young lieutenant you've been assigned graveyard shift as the overnight boat officer. Although you are not the one driving the boat, you are responsible for the safe passage of hundreds of sailors back to their floating hotel—otherwise known as an aircraft carrier—after a long evening of well-deserved in-port recreational activities. The rickety ferry lurches and chugs, flinging the partygoers—your shipmates—to and fro, and it dawns on you that maybe your prescribed summer white uniform of a skirt and three-inch heels was not the best choice for this situation.

But this is your first overseas deployment, and you truly are the "only skirt in the room." None of the guys—none of your leaders— had thought to mention that wearing pants would be a good idea.

MENTORING KEEPS A YOUNG OFFICER, A TEAMMATE, ON THE RIGHT PATH.

White pleated pants were not a required part of my summer white uniform; no women's pants were carried in stock in the ship's store. But a mentor could have taken just a minute to pull me aside—one-on-one, discreet, fast—and say, "Hey, we're going to Hong Kong. If you have to stand the boat officer watch, you'll probably want to wear pants." Mentoring keeps a young officer, a teammate, on the right path. Lesson learned.

Certainly you've been in situations on your leadership journey where having a mentor or someone to give you guidance would've been helpful. According to *Workforce Management*, 76 percent of companies surveyed use mentoring to deliver critical leadership skills. Nearly two-thirds consider mentoring to be effective in leadership development.[51] From Accountemps, 75 percent of Fortune 500 CEOs cited mentoring as one of the top three key success factors in their career.[52]

Mentoring shortens your employees' learning curve and increases productivity. It also builds loyalty. When your teammates or employees feel that you value them enough to invest in their future, they will be less likely to leave your company. This helps you reduce turnover and retain your top performers and high-potential employees; it's a win all around.

* * *

Clearly the importance of effective teamwork and a culture of purpose and trust cannot be overstated. On the flight deck and in the cockpit, our survival and success hinged on teamwork; your organization's success does too. A team that is engaged, that never stops learning and innovating, that can embrace adversity, and that is committed to the mission's success—that is a high-performing team.

How can your achieve the peak performance of your team? By building a culture of continuous improvement. One of the ways to keep your team aligned and continuously learning, improving, and pursuing excellence (even in extreme conditions) is through the process of planning, performing, and progressing successfully to your next goal. We'll cover that in the next chapter.

Chapter 6

PREPARE, PERFORM, PREVAIL

A FOOLPROOF PROCESS FOR HIGH PERFORMANCE

Great leaders are almost always great simplifiers who can cut
through argument, debate, and doubt to offer a solution
everybody can understand.
—*Colin Powell*

On day one of flight school, my fellow naval aviators and I learned something that would permanently change the way we operated. It is a deceptively simple process for conducting the business of flying—or almost any other kind of business. In the tiny briefing room at Naval Air Station Corpus Christi, my on-wing—my first flight instructor— made it clear that there is a precise path to high performance. The hours of classroom instruction before ever stepping foot into a Navy aircraft all drove toward this method. It consists of just a few simple, repeatable steps that would help us plan, execute, and learn from the experience. Today, I've boiled that process down to a simple, straightforward, winning formula: *Prepare. Perform. Prevail.*

Right from the start, it was clear that we were expected to strictly adhere to the method. It became so fundamental to the way we worked that missing even part of one of these steps would cause stress, a feeling that the oversight would definitely come back to bite us. After implementing the process in our daily operations, we came to understand why it received so much emphasis. It provided a way for us to operate at a high level of performance and to keep learning and improving with every success—and every failure. It helped us achieve sustainable results in a situation where an error by any part of the team, from top echelon to lowest rung, could mean loss of life.

Today, many years since I graduated flight school, I still adhere to the Prepare-Perform-Prevail process. For fearless leaders, it is a game changer. If you learn to apply it consistently, it can help you and your team create high-performance results—faster and more efficiently than your competitors. You can have the grandest vision ever, but if you can't execute effectively, if you don't have a plan for the actual doing part—then all that effort is worthless. The Prepare-Perform-Prevail process gives you that plan.

The process is straightforward and precise, easy and elegant. Once you know how to implement it, it will become your secret weapon.

In Phase 1, Prepare, you begin by bringing people together to craft a plan for the operation in question. You continue to Phase 2, Perform, by briefing everyone involved on the plan and executing the plan—this is the doing part. And in Phase 3, Prevail, you come together to debrief—to analyze how things went, and consider how you can do it better next time.

This dynamic process will help make the seemingly impossible, possible. It will allow you to execute your strategy effectively, adapt and adjust quickly, and manage risk. (Naval aviators are world-class risk managers; few other professions in the world take risk as seriously as we do.) And, crucially, it will help you and your people learn to value any failure as a learning opportunity and thus get over your fear of uncertainty and failure—increasing your fearlessness.

Having a straightforward process in place is also reassuring; it allows you to identify greater opportunities in an unpredictable environment. Using this strategy, people know what they need to do, and they have the confidence to move through the steps to successful completion. The same goes for you: You will know what needs to happen when, and you can course-correct when you see the team going astray. The process shows you that you must act in certain simple, repeatable ways. It says, "This is how you do it." The result: more purposeful action and more valuable learning.

The Prepare-Perform-Prevail process also helps you cut through the clutter that so many leaders face. When I talk to people who have recently taken on a new management role, the lion's share of them say they're overwhelmed, bogged down in day-to-day activities. Your vision for the team should serve as a helpful sorting device, but even with a vision, you can find yourself pulled in different directions, wondering which is the best path forward.

This process gives you a road map, shows you the most pressing items, and helps you attack them. It breaks your big goal into pieces you can get started on right away. In chapter 2, we talked about how effective the small-steps approach is for getting where you want to go as a leader. Well, the same is true for your team. The Prepare-Perform-Prevail process lights the path ahead; it engages, involves, and educates those who are going to execute the plan. It calms fear and reluctance because it gives your team a straightforward mechanism to help everyone constantly improve.

In short, when you've got your team following the Prepare-Perform-Prevail process, you can step back and breathe easy for a moment, confident that everyone knows not just what you're working toward but how to get there.

This process works in any type of organization. It will work for you whether you are an executive launching a global, go-to-market strategy . . . an account manager of a sales team . . . a bank manager . . . a restaurant owner . . . a football coach . . . or a floor manager at a production facility. There's no task too big or too small. I've used the Prepare-Perform-Prevail with one of the largest utility companies in the United States, and I use it all the time with my kids—before every volleyball game, motocross race, or basketball game. Perhaps best of all, it takes just thirty seconds: What's the objective? What are we going to work on, and what could get in our way? See you at the finish line! Straightforward. Boom! Done.

Let's cut through the noise—all the information floating around about management, execution, and error reduction—and learn a straightforward system that really works.

Phase I: Prepare

Dwight Eisenhower once said, "In preparing for battle I have always found that plans are useless, but planning is indispensable." Ah, a man after my own heart. Too often, organizations and individuals will spend time crafting a mission statement or holding endless meetings . . . and then just start executing. They miss a crucial step: the Prepare phase, where the team creates and shares its plan.

I hear from organizations several different reasons why they don't take the time to plan:

- *Everyone knows our strategy.*
- *We don't need to plan. We are a creative group and need flexibility.*
- *Strategy? Planning? Ugh! That happens behind closed doors.*
- *We're too busy doing the work of running the company.*

That last one gets me every time.

Want to know the real reasons teams don't plan? Either they don't understand the value, they don't know how to do it, or they want immediate gratification—they want the payoff, and they want it *now*. Yet all those reasons are unfounded. I've seen again and again how even a small, dedicated amount of effective planning can save a ton of execution errors down the road.

By choosing not to plan, you are choosing failure—and mediocrity. And that's if you're lucky! Effective planning is one of the cornerstones of high performance in all environments; without it, you risk surpassing mediocrity and reaching poor quality—if you're lucky. High-performance athletes, sports teams, medical professionals, musicians, and businesses all dedicate time to planning in order to perform error-free under incredible pressure.

I want to be clear: Planning is not the same as having a meeting. Planning is taking the necessary steps that force you to focus very clearly on your mission objective—on how you define *success* and what things should look like when the smoke clears. Because once you start to engage, whether this means you are airborne, in your manufacturing facility, or launching a new marketing plan, things change. They always do.

If you've taken the time beforehand to think through all possible scenarios—the potential threats and obstacles—your chances of responding successfully to change are greatly improved, even if the plan isn't perfect, which it will *never* be. You have to learn to execute with a "good enough" plan—we called this the "80 percent solution." You will not always have 100 percent of the information you need. Things change. Time keeps marching on. Start executing your "good enough" plan so you are not at the mercy of an environment that is outpacing your plan.

Planning for Buy-in

Planning for a large-scale tactical aircraft strike aboard an aircraft carrier is a complex, dynamic process that involves many players, so it's absolutely crucial that we include everyone in the process and create buy-in across the board. As we plan, we seek help from aviators, teammates from different squadrons and military branches, and subject matter experts in weaponeering, intelligence, and even weather forecasting. Planning the mission is very interactive; it doesn't happen in some secret room among only a chosen few. We want to hear from different stakeholders and generate as many ideas and solutions as possible. Each squadron representative has a particular expertise, and this allows a large group to brainstorm and come up with the best possible plan.

By bringing everyone together in a brainstorm, the Navy ensures that multiple points of view pop up. From these alternatives, the team selects the best course of action—what the best weapons are, what the timing should be, how to avoid and suppress the threat. After this rough plan is developed, it is reviewed by the commander of the air group (CAG), who addresses any questions, suggestions, or contingencies. Once the feedback from the CAG is addressed and/ or incorporated, the strike team leader tasks all members to plan their portion. Plans are extraordinarily valuable, but the planning *process* is as important as the *product,* because when everyone is involved, the result is both understanding and buy-in.

When you create buy-in, everyone involved in execution, from the C-suite to the frontline worker, understands the strategy. This is critical. Ask yourself: How many times have you seen your planning process short-circuited, and your team unable to execute effectively or get the ball down the field, because you couldn't get your people 100 percent onboard? When you fail to get results, it's not because the plan or the solution was wrong, but because there wasn't consensus on how to get the job done. In business, as in aviation, the force that eliminates apathy and inertia is buy-in.

This takes time. To come up with the best solution, you need to plan in an environment that values open discussion and counterpoint. You want to embrace the collective wisdom and knowledge of the team, an understanding that the answers may not necessarily come entirely from the most senior or experienced members. But most of all you want your wingman, your coworkers, or your teammates to commit to the decision and agree on how to move forward. You don't have time for the meek, go-along-to-get-along folks or for those who will leave the planning room and start ripping the plan to shreds at the water cooler. You want synergy and buy-in, and you get it by involving everyone in the planning process.

The Power of the Checklist

The best way to develop a comprehensive plan time and again, no matter the mission, is to use a checklist. Naval aviators use checklists for everything, which ensures effective execution of even the most routine tasks: preflight, starting our jets, taking off, landing. We want to make sure no critical tasks are missed or dropped. Our strike-planning checklist is twelve pages long! We are human; we forget things—sometimes even the really important things. But not if we use a checklist.

In the business world, you can use checklists to improve execution of almost any "mission": a sales call, patient safety, project management, employee training. You probably don't need a twelve-page checklist; instead, you can adopt the one we use for our day-to-day flight planning. Below is an example of this tactical planning checklist. It is straightforward, and you can use it in your organization, for virtually any operation your business could undertake. From Wall Street to Wichita, in the operating room or on the manufacturing floor, this works.

1. *Establish the mission objective.* Ask, "What does this project look like at the end state?" Whether you're a project manager, a chief marketing officer, or a sales account manager, the objective should be clear, measurable, achievable, and worthy of your team's effort.
2. *Ask, "Has anyone ever done this before?"* You want to find lessons already learned so you don't make the same mistakes. Reusing knowledge can save time, energy, and money.
3. *Analyze resources versus threats.* What assets do you have that might aid in achieving a successful outcome? What are the greatest threats that stand between your team and success? (Not enough people? Team doesn't have the right skills? Not enough time? Spread too thin?)

4. *Map out the "launch plan."* What is your course of action? What steps will you take to achieve success?

5. *Ask, "What if?"* Plan for contingencies—surprises, risks, weaknesses, lack of funding, too few people, lack of resources, etc.

6. *Involve a "red team."* Get someone or some group of teammates who are not involved in the planning processes to poke holes in what you've laid out.

7. *Plan to debrief.* This is always part of preflight planning. If you don't schedule for feedback (the debrief) up front, chances are slim that you will actually follow through and take the time to debrief post-execution.

Thanks to effective open planning and a tactical checklist, your teammates will now understand what is expected of them.

Review your plans often. Take a hint from TOPGUN: The legendary fighter weapons school reviews its flying and training plans daily to stay on track.

Planning for Contingencies

During the Prepare phase, as you are developing your plan, you need to consider the potential barriers to success. What are the roadblocks that could stand in the way of great execution?

Now, clearly, contingency planning doesn't mean that you *intend* for things to go wrong. But if it happens, you have briefed your team, and everybody knows what to expect and how to behave. This is risk management at its finest.

Imagine being the supplier of power and generators for a large marathon, concert, or other event. A tornado strikes the location after you've already rolled your equipment on station. Do you have a plan to reallocate those assets? Will you be able to communicate if your power goes down? Too often I hear people say in the planning phase, "Yeah, let's not talk about that—that'll never happen." They fail to do the necessary contingency planning. Most businesses don't do this well, if they even do it at all.

That's not the way we operated on the carrier. We did everything we could to think about what could go wrong. We would "What if?" things to death, because we didn't want to be trying to solve these problems while airborne at 500 knots. Instead, we did it while we were still on the ground. We planned for it. Fighter pilots don't like surprises—nor should you.

Planning for contingencies requires *attention to detail*—one of the most common phrases heard throughout Aviation Officer Candidate School was *attention to detail*—a necessity when you're in the preparation stage of execution. Early on in the AOCS program, each of us was given custody of a trusty old M-1 Garand rifle. It became our responsibility to become proficient at disassembling, cleaning, and reassembling the weapon and performing close-order drill for hours, mistake-free. This simple rifle was one of the first tools that the USMC drill instructors used to drive home the importance of attention to detail. God help you if you were the candidate who accidently left a rifle unsecured while at class, out on a run, or at water survival. The chances of finding all of your stuff—and your roommate's stuff—out on the lawn of the AOCS Battalion buildings were pretty high. Even worse was when the DI found a speck of rust or a piece of fuzz or lint clinging to the rifle in a place you didn't even know existed.

But this rigor set the tone for what would be expected of us further down the road: a much greater level of responsibility than taking care of a crappy, old, used weapon. In order to survive in naval aviation, you had to pay meticulous attention to detail, even when—or *especially* when—operating under extraordinarily difficult circumstances.

It's the little things that get you, so make sure to work those little things into your plan. I learned early on in my career to perform even the smallest and most seemingly irrelevant tasks with a commitment to excellence and an eye for the small stuff. In business, too, there are no truly "big things"—only the constant accumulation of little things that need to be done at a high level of execution. If you don't pay attention to detail in the planning phase, how can you expect your teammates to do so?

> THERE ARE NO TRULY "BIG THINGS"—ONLY THE CONSTANT ACCUMULATION OF LITTLE THINGS THAT NEED TO BE DONE AT A HIGH LEVEL OF EXECUTION.

You've probably heard the saying "You play like you practice." In the Navy, we train aggressively for every contingency, every scenario imaginable, so there are no surprises. Nothing is left to chance. We always say, "Train like you fight and fight like you train." We want to show up "at the merge"—the point of conflict, when you're beak to beak with another airplane—with as much confidence as possible. True confidence comes from proper preparation and hard work.

Briefing the Team

Once the bulk of the planning is complete, the next task in the Prepare phase is briefing the team—those who will be involved in the execution of the plan. In the best-case scenario, those who will be executing have been involved already in the planning. But if not, this is the right time to go over the plan and define responsibilities. This is the final walk-through before execution.

By briefing your team members, you are setting them up for success. During the briefing, you should clearly articulate the mission objective, assign roles and responsibilities, analyze potential threats, and discuss contingencies and emergency procedures.

In the Navy, it didn't matter whether we were going out on just a short practice flight—a field carrier landing at our home base—or on a combat air patrol. Before each and every flight, we took the time to brief our team—always. Whether it was a flight of two or a group of forty airplanes launching, the brief was integral to our success and safety. The briefing usually followed a standard format, adjusted slightly for shipboard operations. This was how we made sure everyone knew their roles and responsibilities. The briefing drove a common understanding of the situation and of our objectives; it encouraged buy-in about the plan and how it should be executed. This was an eyeball check—a face-to-face briefing—where we answered all questions and set our team up for success.

You can do this with your team as well. Before a shift change, a big meeting with a client, or a new product roll-out, take the time to walk through the expectations of everyone involved, clarifying roles and responsibilities as you do. You want to make sure everyone has a common understanding of the situation and of the preferred and expected outcome. This doesn't have to be a long briefing—it could take fifteen minutes or an hour. You just want clarity for all team members; you want to answer any last-minute questions.

The three biggies to consider when giving a brief are: time management; a logical, chronological flow; and accurate descriptions of the mission objectives and individual roles and responsibilities, so there is no confusion whatsoever. Here's how this works in the world of naval aviation.

Our preflight briefs are done just prior to our scheduled takeoff time, and typically not much more than an hour is available. Part of running an effective brief is being able to effectively manage this time; briefings do not have the luxury of going on forever or until the briefer decides to stop talking. You need to format or organize your brief in such a way that you cover all the important stuff within a set amount of time.

Part of being a fearless leader hinges on your ability to communicate effectively. Assuming your teammates understand the vision of your organization, their ability to successfully execute will depend on how well they understand your mission objective, their roles, and what is expected of them—how they will impact the success of the team.

In order to gain alignment it is important to take the time to brief your team. Depending on your work cycle, this could be daily, weekly, monthly, and/or quarterly. A briefing should always cover certain elements:

1. *Overview:* What is the overall situation? Give your teammates a quick overview of the current circumstances so they clearly understand the context in which they are operating and the importance and urgency of the task at hand.

2. *Mission objective:* What is your goal? Be precise. There is no room for fuzzy objectives in a high-performing team.

3. *Execution objectives:* What are the overall objectives? What are the roles and responsibilities of every team member? Leave no doubt; vague roles can kill successful execution. (Ever hear someone say, "Well, I thought so-and-so was taking care of that"? Yeah, me too.)

4. *Operational risk management:* What are the mission risks? How do you mitigate the risks you can't eliminate? What are your contingencies? How do you anticipate change or disruptions?

5. *Administration and logistics:* Who will be providing resources and support? Explain the roles of any other people or divisions, either internal or external to your team.

6. *"Flight" conduct and communications:* How will you be communicating as a team? Via email? Via phone? How often—at specified times, when deadlines are met, or when problems are encountered? Be specific. Don't leave your communications to chance.

7. *Questions:* Ensure clarity among your teammates by asking for questions—but not until the end of your brief. Do not allow the constant peppering of questions or the random interruption of your brief; *you* must control the pace or flow of information. There should be no confusion about what is expected during execution. If you have people huddling after your brief, that means you haven't clearly briefed your team.

Once you start integrating a regular, structured briefing process, your team will start to get comfortable with the rhythm and pace of your communication style. You will be able to transfer accurate information anywhere, anytime, much more effectively. In the military, if we don't brief our teams successfully, people are at risk of not coming home.

The Navy's standard operating procedures, which spell out in great detail how a task is to be completed each and every time, are a huge asset in the briefing process. They can be revisited and revised regularly to ensure that there are no misunderstandings on how the plan will be executed. Similarly, in the business world, the importance of good, well-thought-out SOPs cannot be underestimated. The SOPs establish expectations of how the team will behave during execution in order to ensure a job well done or a safe, efficient flight.

Briefing the SOPs brings the team together, even if they have never flown or worked together before. But procedures need to be logical and make sense, or your team won't adhere to them. Without standardized SOPs and strict adherence to them, pilots or team members start to do their own thing—they "wing it." And this is where the mishap rate starts to skyrocket. The best SOPs have been developed with help from the crew force, so they have buy-in and don't feel as though this is just another inane procedure being shoved down their throat.

Of course, SOPs and briefings don't preclude a pilot from exercising good judgment and taking the initiative to assure a safe flight or get the job done. But they do clarify the various responsibilities of all the individuals involved and ensure that everyone is clear on what the mission objective is.

An ideal briefing follows a set formula, although the content and delivery differ widely, of course, depending on your company, your team, and your mission. But all briefs should incorporate and embrace the elements of the Prepare phase: buy-in, a tactical checklist, planning for contingencies, attention to detail, clear objectives, and standard operating procedures.

Here's an example: At the beginning of every shift, every day, at every Ritz-Carlton property, a fifteen-minute staff briefing takes place. The briefing includes the sharing of a "wow" story—a description of great things that have been accomplished while serving the customer *(mission, synergy, buy-in)*. And each briefing reinforces one of the twelve "Service Values" incorporated into the company's Gold Standards. Ritz-Carlton teammates discuss the importance of these values and not only why they matter, but how each employee can make a difference *(buy-in, attention to detail)*. This type of briefing allows Ritz-Carlton to inspire and engage the team, while defining and reinforcing the company's culture and values.[53]

Depending on your role, it may not make sense for you personally to brief your team every day. A weekly, monthly, or even annual briefing can help achieve your teams' goals in terms of preparation. Recently I was a keynote presenter for an amazing Canadian company, Garda Cash Logistics. In an effort to get the team aligned and all singing from the same sheet of music, the company brought a huge contingent off-site to brief the team on the company's goals and objectives. It was one of the best meetings I've seen. The CEO clearly briefed his team and laid out his vision for the company. He explained the specific mission, goals, and objectives; what challenges the current environment presented; what contingency plans were in the works; and how each person would play a critical role in the company's long-term success. Just as important, he asked for input from the team about what was working and what wasn't.

IF YOU WANT TO EXECUTE EXCELLENTLY, YOU CAN'T TAKE ANY SHORTCUTS IN PREPARATION.

This picture-perfect example of a solid briefing followed by an open discussion encouraged team members to share both invaluable lessons learned from the field and recommendations for improvement going forward. The CEO also took the necessary time to praise the great work that the team was already doing. All this together created an enormous amount of synergy and buy-in, and the team has since been able to accelerate its business performance.

Excellence in execution was our goal in aviation—it should be yours in business. And if you want to execute excellently, you can't take any shortcuts in preparation.

Phase 2: Perform

Once you have prepared effectively, it's time for the Perform phase of Prepare-Perform-Prevail. It's time to put away fear and doubt, and just *do*. Great execution will depend on your ability to jump in, start executing, and adhere to your plan, making minor adjustments as necessary.

For a fighter pilot, speed is life. You must make decisions quickly. You must take the initiative and push the envelope, or you will be left behind. As necessary as planning is, we can't extend that phase of the process, overthinking things and getting stuck in "analysis paralysis." If you've prepared thoroughly, what reason could you possibly have for holding back? We have to execute despite fear of failure. As hockey superstar Wayne Gretzky reminds us, "You miss one hundred percent of the shots you don't take."

One execution begins, we can't just mindlessly carry out the plan. Danger lurks ahead. You're going to start encountering those contingencies you (hopefully) planned for, but there will always be ones you didn't foresee. And there will be human error, too. We all make mistakes, even highly trained professionals. More than 80 percent of all civilian and military aviation mishaps are due, at least in part, to pilot error.[54] Expect that both you and your people will have blunders and slip-ups along the way.

This inevitability of mistakes doesn't mean you can't take measures to reduce the likelihood. Understanding why we are prone to making mistakes is the first step in error reduction—and world-class execution. As we discuss the Perform phase, we're going to focus on the quickest way to derail execution: overloading yourself or your teammates with tasks. Once we see why task overload is such a threat—and how you can identify it in your team members—we'll explore how to recognize and combat it.

Understanding Task Overload

We've all experienced the frustration, the stress, and the sinking feeling that come from realizing we face more demands than we can handle at one time—in the cockpit or in the office. Task overload usually takes one of two forms: *technical skill overload* or *information overload.*

Technical skill overload results when our brain fails to prioritize inputs and our mind focuses on a single thing in an attempt to stabilize the situation. The Department of Defense's Human Factors Analysis and Classification System calls this *channelized attention* and defines it as "focusing all conscious attention on a limited number of environmental cues to the exclusion of others of a subjectively equal or higher or more immediate priority, leading to an unsafe situation."[55] This singular focus is the number one human factor associated with the loss of situational awareness and the resulting aviation mishaps.

Information overload, also affectionately known as TMD (Too Much Data) Syndrome, happens when the sheer mass and number of inputs overwhelm the brain's ability to sort and comprehend. A Harvard psychologist reviewing experiments by a number of cognitive psychologists discovered that the maximum number of cues we can attend to simultaneously is seven, plus or minus two.[56] This is not a lot of capacity.

Consider the requirements of flying a Tomcat through a steep turn: control pressure feel, pulling back on the stick, rates of change of bank angle, pitch, altitude, airspeed, air traffic controllers, bells and whistles . . . *Ack!* As you can imagine, in basic flight maneuvers, we are at—or in some cases, beyond—the cognitive task overload point, just from flying a steep turn.

Add a bit of stress, a little fear, or some anxiety to the mix, and the average person's ability to multitask goes right out the window. Stress can narrow the perceptual field, limiting the ability to process new information. It can reduce working memory capacity and inhibit information recall and long-term memory. In what's known as the "strong but wrong" effect, stress can even cause you to revert to previously learned behaviors that may or may not be effective. Collectively, this conspires to thwart your ability to get the darn job done. You are dangerously close to being unable to execute your well-thought-out plan.

But fighter pilots have developed coping mechanisms, techniques, and tricks that allow us to work through extraordinarily high task loads while under extreme stress. The military has spent a lot of time and money researching and mitigating task overload over the years, and the most surprising thing discovered early on was that typically, pilots weren't even aware of its onset. They would reach cognitive overload and hit the ground (literally crash!) before they even knew what was happening.

Task overload is so common that naval aviators include the subject in our preflight briefings, pointing out exactly when during a particularly challenging mission it is most likely to occur. This awareness helps you and your wingman recognize when you are becoming task-overloaded.

To effectively deal with task overload, you must be able to identify it when it starts. In the heat of the moment, however, the three major telltale symptoms of overload are easy to miss:

1. *Shutting down:* In the face of a seemingly impossible situation, you simply flee. You've worked with people who have reached this stage; you've seen their arms go up in the air as they yell, "I've had it! I quit! I'm done!" Or you've seen how others completely close in and get unusually quiet.

2. *Compartmentalizing:* You shut down certain parts of the brain in an attempt to focus on just one thing at a time. By denying or repressing certain things, however, you are ignoring the essential big picture. You might miss tasks; your work may become erratic and inconsistent.

3. *Channelizing:* You focus on one thing to the total exclusion of all others. In this situation, pilots may miss radio calls, fail to see other airplanes, and so forth. You might see channelized attention in aviators who are in the midst of target fixation, which typically happens when a pilot is nose-down, pointed toward the ground, on a diving target run at 500 knots. He or she is focused—too focused—and may forget to actually fly the jet. With eyes on the target, the pilot flies the jet straight at it—and straight into the ground. That's called "dying relaxed." Similarly, in the business world, we have such a tight focus on the task at hand that, oftentimes to our peril, we ignore incoming phone calls or repeated texts—all of which may be important.

Think task overload and channelized attention happen only when you're airborne? Recently, four Air Force F-16s were taxiing to the runway, when one plane rear-ended another. The pilot of the first aircraft had stopped on the taxiway to do a standard check of his radar. The second and third aircraft stopped behind him. The fourth aircraft was busy doing aircraft systems checks and failed to realize the plane in front of him had stopped. The offending aircraft received damage totaling more than $2 million; the third aircraft in the formation had almost $600,000 worth of damage. The accident investigation found that there was a breakdown in visual scan, task misprioritization, and channelized attention.

The symptoms of task overload are recognizable in the business arena, too. Recently, as a large pharmaceutical company went through a "rightsizing" period, suddenly there were far fewer people to accomplish all the same tasks. The remaining employees were worked into the ground, and their productivity plummeted. The company also saw a 40 percent spike in sick leave during the first six months following the rightsizing. Overwhelmed by the workload, people were just shutting down.

The lesson: Always be vigilant about task overload among your teammates. This awareness can help your team avoid mishaps, whether it's a "fender bender" or a midair collision of epic proportions.

Once you understand *why* we are prone to making mistakes in our execution, particularly under stressful conditions, and can spot when task overload is happening, the next step is to mitigate the risks. We can do this by following one of the golden rules of flying, a lesson that we learned our first day of flight school: aviate, navigate, and communicate.

Aviate, Navigate, Communicate

In training to fly into the enemy's integrated air defense systems, we had to fly very low to the ground at very high speeds: one hundred to two hundred feet off the deck at 500 miles per hour. If you make a mistake at this speed and altitude, you are less than one second from dying. Clearly, it is crucial for aviators to prioritize our tasking in this environment. We have a finite capacity for how much information and tasking we can handle at any given time. We have to be sure that we don't hit the ground while we are also running our weapons systems, communicating with our wingman, navigating toward a target, and keeping an eye out for enemy surface-to-air missiles. How did we develop the skills to cope with this intense workload, and to prioritize and focus on several important tasks all at once? Aviate, navigate, communicate—a simple process that can work for you, too.

Aviate

First things first: Focus on what matters. At the end of the day you have to aviate—just fly the airplane. You have to maintain control, get the plane stable, and keep it safe. Without this first step, nothing else really matters.

Similarly, in business, when a crisis pops up and people feel overloaded, the first thing you must do is slow down and make sure the team is stable, safe, and operational. Often when we are panicked, we get time compressed—time seems to speed by, out of control. We can handle this by "hacking the clock" during a crisis—noting the time and possibly even slowing things down for a period of hours or days—you can maintain a more realistic perspective. What are your organization's main priorities? Get all the information by pulling the team together to get a sense of the scope of the problem. Observe, listen, and ask questions. Focus on what matters. Maintain control. Fly your airplane.

Navigate

Once you've returned to your inner compass and things are stable, figure out where you need to go. If you're going to fly, you've got to know where you are going. Even if you are out on a routine mission, you still need a plan for where you are going and how you'll get there. In a crisis, once you've got a sense for the stability of things, or at least an idea of how quickly things are coming unglued, you must set a course for action. You must plan your next step: Where are you going to go from here?

When you're flying a jet, your first step in an emergency is to stop losing altitude and get your nose headed in the right direction. Remember your plan? It's time to review your tiny details, what-ifs, and contingency plans.

What's the solution? Who can help you? The key here is to stay s-l-o-w-e-d d-o-w-n. The time you spend in deliberate assessment will pay off as you resume navigating forward. I've worked with a lot of executives who are dealing with a crisis and the resultant task overload, and I have seen many a business leader pull out of a nosedive by slowing things down for a couple of hours or even a couple of days to get it right.

Communicate

Now that you are safely headed in the right direction and out of extremis, communicate your intentions to the team: "Here's the problem, and here is what we are going to do about it. These few things are your priority tasks right now." Contact others to ask for help if necessary. (If you don't get the first two steps right, of course, all the talking in the world won't get you out of trouble—so keep your priorities straight!)

Fighter pilots aren't born with the ability to prioritize tasks in a high-stress environment; we learn the skills necessary to do so. We learn to work through the strain and tension of task overload by using this simple, three-pronged message of Aviate-Navigate-Communicate. And we practice this relentlessly: in preparation, in briefing, in simulators, in flight, and in our day jobs. You can use these same tools and techniques to greatly improve your execution—even in a crisis.

Phase 3: Prevail

You've now prepared and performed as you lead your team toward achieving your business objective—but does that mean you're done? Far from it! In fact, you could argue that the third and final phase in the Prepare-Perform-Prevail process is the most critical. The heart of the third phase is the debrief, where you bring everyone together to review the first two phases, assess what went right and what went wrong, root out the mistakes, and identify lessons learned that will help you improve performance for the next operation. The Prevail part of the process is a hallowed learning environment where rank has no privilege and honest feedback is paramount. The objective is to learn from successes and failures that happened during the Perform step and to use that information to Prevail now and in the future.

The Prevail step is a fighter pilot's secret weapon to ensure high performance. The technique has been refined over hundreds of thousands of hours and decades of flying. Examining the results of planning and performance has saved countless lives and dramatically reduced the military aviation mishap rate. Not only that, but it allows for rapid improvement among this and the next generation of pilots. In the Navy, we debrief immediately, following each and every flight.

Why? Because it is that critical. We must review the details of our performance in order to stay alive and improve—and the details get murkier the longer you wait.

Even if the team executes the plan well, there's always something that could be done better, more effectively, more efficiently. And, as we all know, sometimes things go completely off the rails. No matter where you are on that

A CULTURE OF EXCELLENCE MEANS YOU NEVER STOP LEARNING.

success spectrum, it's vital that everyone debrief after the execution, assessing how the previous phases went and identifying the take-aways. That's how you create a culture of excellence the never lets you stop learning.

Your chances of long-term success are greater when you incorporate the Prevail step. Why? Because debriefing allows you to identify any shortfalls or gaps in performance sooner than your competition does—and trust me, if your enemy is smart, they are already debriefing based on their encounter with you. By uncovering new opportunities faster, however, your team becomes more agile, adapting and adjusting to changing market conditions faster than the competition. Debriefing after a mission can even improve your ability to anticipate your next move—and the competition's.

When debriefing is performed regularly, preferably face-to-face (although via telephone or videoconference works well too), it keeps the organization focused on learning and continuous improvement. Whether you are debriefing a go-to-market plan, a sales plan, or a product rollout, the debrief is crucial for analyzing not only your execution, but how effective and well understood your plan was.

You can determine this by figuring out the answers to the following five questions:

1. What was supposed to happen?
2. What actually happened?
3. Why were there differences?
4. What can we learn?
5. How can we incorporate that lesson into execution next time?

The debrief is vastly underutilized by leaders in corporate America, although peak performers use it with regularity because it is terribly effective; they understand that it's one of the fastest ways to build trust and drive continuous improvement within your team. The goal is to improve performance, of course—but people still avoid the debrief because they fear their performance being assessed. They shy away from accountability. If you are building a culture of excellence, however, the debrief is a powerful tool that can actually save you time in the long run by preventing execution errors. Take the time to debrief at the end of each project . . . after an unexpected event . . . during a lengthy rollout implementation. Trust me, it's worth the time, no matter how busy you are. Taking the time to improve actually *gives you time back* in the end by reducing all of the execution errors and fire fighting.

> THE DEBRIEF IS ONE OF THE FASTEST WAYS TO BUILD TRUST AND DRIVE CONTINUOUS IMPROVEMENT WITHIN YOUR TEAM.

Depersonalizing the Debrief

The biggest obstacle you'll face as you implement the debrief with your team is when identifying what could've gone better turns into laying blame. Making things personal is the last thing you want. So how do you show everyone where improvements could be made, without focusing on pointing the finger?

You must draw on your fearlessness, and you have to start by admitting your own faults—openly and frequently—in debrief sessions. In chapter 3, we saw how leaders show integrity by owning their faults, and the debrief is the most powerful venue to open up to your people about how you, as a key member of the team, can improve.

Think about what happens in your organization right now when people make mistakes, when they screw up? What *truly* is your culture? Are people afraid to admit mistakes? If so, the debrief process will be crippled.

Make it clear to everyone by stating at the outset of every debrief that the intention of this phase isn't to blame errors on a certain team member. It's not about *who* is right, but *what* is right. Explain that instead the debrief is an emotion-free zone; nothing said is personal— this is simply a group of high-performing individuals coming together as a team to identify how they can take their game to the next level and learn how to do things better.

Be explicit in communicating that the debrief is a safe place where people can talk frankly and openly about their own mistakes. Ego and rank have no place here. For this moment, everyone is on the same level, and everyone has a voice. If you develop a culture that allows people to debrief without getting their feelings hurt, you can learn quicker, create faster, gain an advantage over your competition, and accelerate professional growth and opportunities among your people.

In the Prevail phase, you have to model the culture you seek by keeping your own emotions in check. More than one squadron ready room has experienced heated discussions about what happened in flight. That's okay, as long as it doesn't devolve into personal attacks or disrespect. People need the opportunity to share their perspectives, their opinions about what they saw. If you dismiss or disregard them out of hand because you don't agree with their opinion—or because their view might suggest *you* could have done something better—you could be losing a valuable opportunity to see an important perspective. If you berate or humiliate your people, they won't speak up again.

Putting yourself into the debrief may open you and your leadership approach up to criticism. Nevertheless, maintain your bearing, listen, and keep an open mind, and it will pay you back in spades.

By the same token, you have to provide constructive feedback on your team members' performance, and that's one of the biggest challenges most leaders face. Using constructive feedback instead of personal criticism is important; leaving everyone's self-esteem intact is crucial. But many leaders don't like to do it—they don't feel comfortable critiquing someone's performance, especially face-to-face, and they don't take the time to be good at it. This means the folks who need feedback are either not getting it at all or not receiving it in actionable terms, which leads to frustration because they feel as though they can't do anything right.

As a fearless leader you are responsible for establishing a culture of continuous improvement—a culture of learning—that allows for a good flow of constructive criticism. You must give actionable feedback—information your people can use to improve their performance. Likewise, when you *get* feedback that is unclear, you need to be willing to ask the follow-on questions necessary to turn it into *actionable* feedback.

The Navy Blue Angels do a great job of wrapping up their debrief sessions. Each aviator says, "I made this mistake, and I'll fix it. Glad to be here." Never discount the power of a positive attitude and perpetual optimism. Showing belief in yourself and your capabilities and in those of your team is a force multiplier.

Overcoming Atychiphobia

When the fear of failure (*atychiphobia*) looms overhead, everyone's performance suffers. This is one of the great powers of the debrief: it recasts mistakes as opportunities to improve, reducing the atychiphobia at the heart of so many sluggish, low-performing teams.

The debrief process shows your people that there should be no stigma attached to making mistakes, to failing. After all, if you're never failing, you're probably not doing anything challenging. You're too comfortable—and if you're not pushing yourself, you're never going to reach your potential. When Elie Wiesel, Nobel Laureate and former prisoner in the Auschwitz, Bruna, and Buchenwald concentration camps, was asked if he had any regrets, he replied, "I did not make enough mistakes."

Google is known as a forward-thinking company that bravely forges new ground on a regular basis. When a product fails to reach its potential at Google, they kill the product—but they pull all of its best features into another effort. Gopi Kallayil, Google's chief social evangelist, says, "Failure is actually a badge of honor, and failure is the way to be innovative and successful. You can fail with pride."

As a leader, you must recognize that failures *will occur*. We certainly don't want them to become a trend, but when they do happen, we need to own it and understand what happened. Failure is not permanent; it doesn't paralyze you.

The power of the debrief is that it helps you understand the mechanics of success. It gives you information on how to repeat your wins and, by the same token, how not to repeat your losses. In AOCS, we were given opportunities to succeed and also put in positions where we were guaranteed to fail. We were expected to learn from every experience—certainly from the failures. Learning while doing is a beautiful thing.

Our unspoken debrief was not a formal process, but it went something like this:

- Take responsibility.
- Learn from the experience.
- Apply the lessons learned—*quickly.*
- Accelerate your execution—do better next time!

FEARLESS LEADERS RECOGNIZE THAT FAILURES WILL OCCUR AND THAT THE REAL ENEMY IS NOT FAILURE BUT *FEAR* OF FAILURE.

This was about rapid learning: fail, learn, move on. You can do the same for your team. Emphasize repeatedly that failure isn't a bad thing. It's not a problem that needs to be ferreted out. No one is going to be punished. Tell them that, in fact, failure is a *good* thing—a learning tool. Fearless leaders recognize that failures will occur and that the real enemy is not failure but *fear* of failure.

Capturing Lessons Learned

A Navy airman who has been working on the flight deck of an aircraft carrier is constantly passing along what he has learned to his buddies. Why? Because it could save his life, his buddies' lives, or someone else's life—maybe yours or mine! That's why, in my world, the debrief process is so critical.

After we bravely land our 60,000-pound F-14 Tomcat on the pitching deck of the aircraft carrier in the black of night, and as we are taxied into what will be our jet's parking spot for the night, we have to trust. We are counting on our eighteen-, nineteen-, and twenty-year-old yellow shirts not to taxi us right off the edge. It is so dark we can't see the edge, and that three-inch-tall scupper is the only thing keeping our aircraft from going into the drink before we can eject. We're relying on the more senior crewmen to teach these youngsters everything they can, trusting that there is a constant dialogue and constant learning. We're counting on the lessons learned from the debrief—that is what keeps us all alive and operating on the flight deck.

In carrier aviation, you can execute a landing well—but never perfectly. Every single pass is critiqued and debriefed by the landing signal officers (LSOs), and you're graded, no matter your rank or experience level. A culture of learning and continuous improvement is a hallmark of naval aviation. Guiding all that we do are the ideas of learning before, during, and after our performance.

In business, too, you should wrap up your business debriefs by capturing the lessons learned. These summarized learning points are very valuable—a key element of the Prevail phase. Remember, this is not about blaming people. Think about who else in your organization could benefit from your successes and failures. Reusing lessons learned by colleagues is faster and smarter than making the same mistake twice.

The debriefing process can unearth multiple opportunities for your teammates to provide input; it can be as simple as asking them for it. Too often I work with organizations whose frontline team members have never been asked for their opinion on how something could work better. Worse yet, these people have solutions that they aren't sharing, simply because they think nobody cares. This is such a lost opportunity! Your employees are a treasure trove of fantastic information from the front lines. Don't forget to include them in the conversation!

Starting Your Team's Debrief Process

I've been fortunate enough to walk many teams and organizations through the Prevail phase of execution and, in particular, down the path to successful debriefing. This process works with factory employees, salespeople, and Fortune 10 executives—and it will work for you, your team, and your organization.

When starting your own debrief process, return again and again to the five straightforward questions: *What was supposed to happen? What actually happened? Why were there differences? What can we learn? How can we incorporate that lesson into execution next time?* It takes discipline and personal accountability to do this after every evolution and at the end of every day. At a minimum, take a few minutes at the end of each day to ask *yourself* these questions. Did you hit your goals? Be honest. Don't leave execution excellence to chance. You will not achieve high performance without taking the time to debrief so you can move on toward bigger and better goals.

If you're wondering when to debrief, NFL players offer a great example. Have you ever noticed how quarterbacks, as soon as they come off the field, are already talking to the upstairs booth and looking at images of what just happened? In essence they are debriefing on the fly. They are trying to gain as much asking all the right questions: *What just worked, and why? What didn't, and why not?* They do this even with a minute left in the game—even when their team is ahead!

And though you won't see it on your television screen, you can bet these fearless leaders are looking at video on Monday morning.

You can debrief with your team at any time. Set the rhythm that works for you: weekly, biweekly, at shift changes, after a project has been launched and again after it is completed—whatever makes sense for your organization's needs, whatever matches your activity cycle. The point is, you want your team to be continuously learning, both during execution and afterward.

As you lead your team's debrief, emphasize that team performance is about both individual and mutual accountability, improvement, and commitment to learning. As a fearless leader, it all starts with you. You are the model your teammates will pattern themselves after. You set the tone of the conversation, so you need to begin by setting the stage for success. Once you've established the amount of time for the debriefing session, you should be the first to speak.

Explain the goal of the debrief very clearly at the beginning of the session: to figure out what worked, what didn't, and *why*, so the team can avoid repeating its mistakes and can integrate and apply the things that worked into your next round of execution. Then remind your team that achieving this goal requires transparency and honesty from everyone involved; there are no spectators allowed in the debrief, only those who participated—who had skin in the game.

Next, restate the mission objective, to make sure everyone is clear on what the team was trying to accomplish. If there are discrepancies, that means your initial brief was incomplete—lesson learned.

Continue by offering up something that you, the leader, could improve on in the next go-around. This usually will open up the lines of communication. Keep things positive. Remind your people that

TAKE THE TIME TO IDENTIFY WHAT WORKED, WHAT DIDN'T, AND *WHY*.

this is a learning event; it's a respectful environment, not a monkey poo–throwing event or a blame-and-flame arena.

Never forget that it is just as important to debrief successful events as failures. The reason you should dig deep on these questions is to figure out whether your success was created by luck or by skill. If you just got lucky, that could be disastrous for the next person to fly that mission; you don't usually get lucky twice. So you must take the time to identify what worked, what didn't, and *why*.

Finding out what didn't work requires your attention too. When fighter pilots are operating high-performance machines at the edge of our human limits, the stakes are extremely high and the details matter. Lives are on the line; taxpayer-funded equipment is at risk. So we are relentless in our pursuit of uncovering and identifying the mistakes on every mission. The same is true in business, when company profitability—or survival—is on the line. Your team's future and that of your organization hang in the balance; you can't afford to half-ass your evaluation.

After you discover what went wrong, of course, your next step is figuring out how to fix it. High-performing organizations are constantly learning and improving, never losing sight of the overall team purpose. This is all about pursuing excellence—getting better both on an individual level and as a team. We do that by immediately integrating those takeaways—the lessons learned—into our follow-on execution.

A quote from sociologist Benjamin Barber applies here: "I don't divide the world into the weak and the strong, or the successes and the failures. I divide the world into the learners and non-learners."

*   *   *

Now that you understand the foolproof Prepare-Perform-Prevail process and how to implement it, you're ready to start using it with your team. This process will allow your team to win consistently, even in a changing environment—and constant change is a business reality.

A friend of mine, also a naval aviator, shares this story about implementing the Prepare-Perform-Prevail process:

> I went to work for an oil company recently that had a good crew on a good rig, but it was taking them ten days to move from site to site. I started with a workshop/planning session and requested that the rig leadership as well as superintendents—at a minimum—be there.
>
> No one had ever come in to specifically help the company with rig moves, so the planning took about an hour. In the session *(planning)*, we found multiple differences of opinion between the trucking company, the drilling contractor/ rig owner, and the oil company on how best to move a rig. Together we decided on a course and set some meeting/ update *(brief/debrief)* times.
>
> As we executed the move, some people were unhappy or uncomfortable with some of the changes, even though these changes were not really significant. We gave them a voice in the process and worked through the discomfort.

Throughout the execution phase, we monitored the plan, sought information when changes were noticed, and got all parties involved when big changes were made. We also kept the communication going so that good decisions and adjustments could be made when resources, weather, or milestones changed.

After losing a day to weather and another to unplanned maintenance, we moved the rig in less than seven days—over a 30 percent improvement from their previous average—on the first try, and with no damage to people or equipment!

Prepare. Perform. Prevail. It's the Navy way. It's the TOPGUN way. It is our way of life.

Chapter 7

RESILIENCE

REBOUNDING FROM ADVERSITY

*What lies behind us and what lies ahead of us are tiny
matters compared to what lies within us.*
—Ralph Waldo Emerson

From the late 1950s until 2004, every jet-qualified naval aviator and
almost every naval flight officer went through training in the T-2
Buckeye. Anthony Hahn was a student naval aviator at VT-4, based at
Naval Air Station Pensacola—a man full of life, a man who embodied
optimism, positive attitude, and generosity. He was a great friend of
mine and one of my brother's best friends.

On June 4, 1991, Anthony died after ejecting from his North
American T-2C Buckeye, just north of Pensacola, Florida. At a fairly low
altitude, his aircraft experienced a runaway nose-down trim malfunc-
tion—he went into a sudden dive. Anthony ejected in the nick of time,
but broke both arms. While swinging to the ground in his parachute,
he got tangled up in a tree. With both arms broken, he was unable
to get his oxygen mask off. Anthony suffocated and died in the tree.

This was just over a week before I was scheduled to graduate from AOCS and head to flight school. That warm, sunny day in June, in the chapel at NAS Pensacola, was the first time I heard the Navy Hymn ("Eternal Father, Strong to Save") playing for a friend of mine. It was a day I will never forget, and it was not the last time I would hear and sing those sorrowful words:

Lord, guard and guide the men who fly
Through the great spaces in the sky,
Be with them always in the air,
In dark'ning storms or sunlight fair.
O, hear us when we lift our prayer,
For those in peril in the air . . .

Anthony's accident hit very close to home. Although I didn't question whether I still wanted to fly, there was a part of me that felt shockingly *selfish*. My brother was already partway through flight school, and now our parents had to live with the idea that both of their children could die in an accident like Anthony's. How could I do this to them? There were only the two of us siblings, and having both of your kids in the military *and* in flight school had to be nerve-wracking. During the week of Anthony's funeral service, there were several late-night phone calls with my parents involving quiet tears. But through it all they were steadfast supporters, and I remained focused on what mattered to me: serving my country to the best of my ability.

So to me, June 4, 1991, is not just a random date. It's the date I learned about resilience and the price of living your dream. It was a time of reflection and choice: opt to stay in and press on, or panic, opt out, and walk away. I chose to meet adversity head-on. I saw the challenges and risks clearly, and I kept moving forward with calm determination. Of course, I didn't know at the time that just a few years later, the death of another friend and fellow naval aviator would test me once again—and put me at the center of a media firestorm.

We talked in chapter 2 about tenacity: the commitment required to get through the challenges of leadership. We also talked, in chapter 6, about learning from failure and turning mistakes into opportunities. These character traits act as a foundation for another requirement of fearless leaders: resilience.

Resilience is the ability to withstand, recover, adapt, and grow in the face of stressors and changing demands. Resilience is what you'll need to call upon when you face a major, life-changing circumstance, one you probably didn't see coming and probably didn't cause through any action of your own. Resilience is what you need when everything blows up in your face—when it feels as though you were just hit by a meteor.

I refer to these types of experiences as "crucibles," and every person faces them in life. They are traumatic, life-changing events that end up forming the way you lead—and the way you live. They shape what you believe to be possible about yourself and about your team. Crucibles are huge, life-challenging moments. To lead fearlessly, you'll have to develop the resilience to succeed despite them.

Of course, adversity comes in many forms. Every person and organization, at some time, experiences challenges and adversity in life. Overcoming these obstacles can seem insurmountable, too tough to handle. Sometimes these challenges are enough to make us quit right in our tracks. So who barely survives—and who thrives?

Those who are resilient are the ones who thrive.

If you haven't yet experienced your life's crucible, you can learn from understanding others' experiences and stories. Then, when your walls come crashing down, you'll be able to take these lessons and set yourself up for success.

Life wouldn't be life if bad things didn't happen to us. Usually the big stuff hits us out of the blue—a job loss, the death of a loved one, a permanent disability, a miscarriage, a swift economic downturn. It comes from nowhere, and it changes everything. When these situations happen, we have to summon up our resilience. Even when the worst hits us, we have to show ourselves and the world that we can bounce back, emerging even stronger and more committed to success.

This is true, of course, for every human on the planet, but leaders face a special challenge. We put ourselves out there. We go for big goals and swing for the fences. We take responsibility for others—for their lives (in the case of the military) and for their livelihoods (in the case of a business organization). That means there's even more at stake for leaders when a bolt from the blue threatens to knock us off our feet.

When problems or setbacks occur, everyone will be looking at you, the leader, to see how you are going to react. Here's a bit of advice: Do. Not. Panic. Panic-stricken people do not make good decisions, nor do they inspire confidence in their team.

Whether you are in agriculture and dealing with extreme weather challenges . . . in the car manufacturing industry and suddenly having to recall millions of vehicles . . . or part of a healthcare system and trying to work your way through reforms . . . don't panic. Stay focused on what matters, on what is important to you and your team. A changing landscape is normal. There will always be new challenges and "opportunities," if you are able to recognize them. As our drill instructors used to say, "Semper Gumby"—always flexible.

Adversity is not going away anytime soon. Luckily, we don't really want it to. The ability to bounce back when adversity strikes is one of the greatest predictors of long-term success and happiness. If you discover that you can learn from and find real meaning in the trials of life, you'll know that you have what it takes to be a fearless leader. Adversity introduces you to yourself. For any leader or team, how you react—how you respond when the stuff hits the fan—can determine whether you survive and thrive . . . or let circumstances destroy you.

> **ADVERSITY INTRODUCES YOU TO YOURSELF.**

The bad news is that people, in my observation, are becoming less resilient. I hear harsh circumstances trotted out as excuses for low achievement, low expectations, low performance, and not a whisper of personal accountability. We seem to expect that bad things won't happen, that the world should be good to us, that we should be kindly ushered toward success. But that's just not the way it is!

Certainly, some of us face more trying events than others—life is famously unfair, after all. But anyone, in any circumstances, can challenge himself or herself to show resilience when the inevitable bad things happen. In fact, it's usually from these bad experiences that we can take away huge, positive lessons.

In chapter 1, we talked about *additive experiences*—how every leader needs them. Whether it's a risky project or a complex acquisition, these breakthrough experiences—the situations that you're not fully prepared for—are extraordinarily valuable. *But only if you learn from them.* Leading through adversity is a marker of a successful leader. What you learn from overcoming adversity plays a crucial role in your future success.

If you take positive, decisive action, you can improve your capacity to withstand adversity, bounce back from setbacks, and thrive. You can use adversity to regain your focus on what matters, grow your own skill set or perspective, and ultimately use it to empower yourself and your team. But first, you have to get over and through your biggest crucible.

Facing My Biggest Crucible

I had my fair share of roadblocks on the path to the cockpit of the F-14 Tomcat, but none were bigger than the scrutiny and betrayals I faced in the mid-1990s. It's a long, frustrating story filled with a lot of misinformation and misperceptions that still exist—and that I still hope to clarify. But it's also an instructive example of the kind of adversity that many fearless leaders have to confront.

After earning my wings and finishing flight school at the top of my class, I headed west to California, to Naval Air Station Miramar—the home of TOPGUN—otherwise known as Fightertown U.S.A. My hard work had paid off, and my dream to fly the US Navy's premier fighter jet had come true. I arrived at VF-124—the F-14 training squadron—in July 1993, excited to learn how to fly the Tomcat. It wasn't long before I felt the first backlash: the nonsensical commentary directed toward women in combat aviation.

I found out that several lieutenants were testifying to Senate panels, railing against women flying in combat. I didn't get it. I was at the top of my flight school class, so it sounded to me as if these lieutenants would rather fly with people who were less qualified, as long as they had the correct "plumbing." That seemed awfully stupid—crazy stupid, in fact. It defied all common sense.

Under extraordinary scrutiny, I finished my initial training for the F-14, and it was time to head to my fleet squadron. Typically each squadron has a twelve-month workup schedule that involves a lot of time away from home: time spent training, flying on and off the aircraft carrier, and doing large-scale airwing training exercises in Fallon, Nevada. Through it all, our squadron learned to prepare, perform, and prevail. Together.

During one of the training cycles at the aircraft carrier, an event occurred that would dramatically change the environment in terms of acceptance of female Navy pilots across the United States. On October 25, 1994, Kara Hultgreen, the other female aviator in my squadron, had a fatal mishap while approaching the aircraft carrier. I heard the news as I was sitting in my F-14, about to taxi out of the chocks to launch out to the aircraft carrier, only about an hour behind her. That mishap immediately became a lightning rod for both sides of the women-in-combat issue.

The tragedy caused an onslaught of media attention. And for a variety of reasons completely unrelated to me, the environment became horribly, unbelievably hostile. In the wake of Kara's death, accusations of unfairness and special treatment flew back and forth, with intense emotions on all sides. For example, the Navy went to extraordinary lengths to recover the wreckage of Kara's aircraft off the ocean floor—something they hadn't done before. Was the recovery because she was a female or because of the critical interest in why the mishap occurred? I'm not sure. Either way, it caused angst within the squadrons; nobody could understand why other mishaps at sea did not appear to be so thoroughly investigated.

To add to the disquiet, Secretary of the Navy John Dalton attended Kara's burial service in Arlington, Virginia. It was the first time anybody ever recalled the secretary of the Navy showing up for a lieutenant's funeral. What wasn't explained in the media or in the squadrons, however, was that he was there in a personal capacity: He and Kara's mom were lifelong friends. That information was never passed along, and the *perception* of special attention and special treatment pushed all the wrong buttons for many people.

To certain people, this was a morale crusher—it made them feel less valuable. And I get that. Would SecNav have shown up at their funerals if they crashed? Sadly, probably not. (But in my opinion, the Secretary of the Navy or some other high-ranking officer should show up at every soldier's funeral.)

This is an example of where fearless leadership matters: stepping up to the plate, sharing information, having uncomfortable conversations. Otherwise, gossip-mongering, anonymous comments, and ill will can permeate your team. Had the commander of the airwing stepped up to the plate to fully explain the situation, some of those hard feelings could've been avoided. But it wasn't done. In the midst of a large-scale cultural change—integrating women into the airwings—communication and transparency were critical. A team's culture in an airwing is critical; it must be based on trust, mutual support, and inclusivity. The lack of information did nothing to sustain this culture.

Now, of course, I was thrust into the spotlight as the remaining female F-14 pilot—and everyone was watching me. They were watching to see if I would crack, cry, or show any emotion whatsoever. God knows, I was already in the position of having to manage perceptions. What if I was too emotional? "Chicks can't handle it," people would say.

What if I got angry? "Ah, yes—she's *bossy*."

If I maintained a Swiss-neutral, detached presence? "She must not care."

The scrutiny before Kara's death had been intense, but I was in no way prepared for this. Yes, I had lost friends to aviation mishaps before—too many already. But when they crashed, *my* skills weren't immediately called into question. I had no experience in dealing with this type of jacked-up situation.

I took no time off and talked to no one about this, and really no one in my squadron asked too many questions. What could they say? They knew it was a bad situation. We all were unprepared.

So I had reached the pinnacle of success: I was an operational combat fighter pilot. I had earned my spot through years of performance and practice. But what I didn't know was that I was about to get the rug yanked out from underneath me. I was about to get T-boned. Jackhammered. Blindsided.

Six months later, when I was deployed on cruise, things got really ugly. Unbeknownst to me at the time, information was released to a lobbyist that makes her living attacking military women in nontraditional roles, especially women in combat. Her main ammunition was the accusation that we were not qualified. Now, this lady is a paid lobbyist. She and her husband make lots of money every year by attacking military women. That was the biggest issue in her arsenal. And in the months following Kara's mishap, this zealot lobbyist published a false report against me. It claimed that I was not qualified to fly the F-14, that I had never even finished my training—which, of course, I had.

The report appeared in newspapers across the country and around the world. It was all over the ship. Copies were faxed to every possible onboard location—and to every Department of Defense installation *worldwide*. As in, everywhere.

Think about that for a second: You're twenty-five years old, you're in the combat theater, and you're getting slaughtered in the press with no way to defend yourself. There are newspaper articles out there, smearing your name. All of your peers see it. The leadership chain sees it. Remember, this is not the era of instant-access Internet. There is no Twitter, no Facebook. There are no embedded reporters. The "reporting" in the major newspapers is the only news people get—and it's dragging your name through the mud. What do you do?

To say this experience was devastating would be a gross understatement. I still can't find the words to sufficiently articulate how damaging it was.

This "information" being passed around wasn't true.

I think the lobbyist thought that by going after me—a very visible target as the only female Tomcat pilot—she could slow down the inevitable upward progress of women in military aviation. Because why would anyone else dare to step into the ring if they could expect this kind of vicious attack? What other woman would have the heart to dare break through a glass ceiling, *or even dare to contribute,* if she was going to get gutted publicly?

Unfortunately for me, the leadership chain chose not to handle this public attack. No one stood up publicly and said, "This isn't true! Don't believe it!" And to make things even worse, this bad publicity—even though it was false—came on the heels of Tailhook and was tangled up in all of the previous negative publicity.

Soon after arriving on station in the Persian Gulf, I was grounded—pulled from the cockpit and sent home. I count that time as one of the toughest periods of my life. It was also a period of time during which I learned a tremendous amount about myself; about the importance of being able to stand up not only for yourself, but for others who don't have a voice; and about the importance of having a supportive network and advocates in your corner.

But most of all, I learned exactly how to be resilient.

The Real Story

After an extensive investigation, the Navy found I should never have been grounded. Although they offered to send me back to the Tomcat, I declined. Hard to believe, but I did. My reputation had been dragged through the mud—how could I go back? I was also offered a spot to fly the F-18 Hornet. But there was a catch—there always is, isn't there? In order to avoid the appearance of giving me "preferential treatment" by putting me "ahead" of other students who had been in a pool—waiting to start training—the Navy determined that it would be up to eighteen months before I would even see the inside of the cockpit. Why was the whole "preferential treatment" thing a big deal? Because the lobbyist who attacked Kara posthumously, and who then went after me, had alleged that Kara and I had received preferential treatment in our training.

So what really happened that led to this original allegation of "preferential treatment"? And why was it so wrong?

After I had graduated from flight school and earned my Wings of Gold, I was given orders to the West Coast F-14 FRS, the training squadron. The first airwing to be deployed *with women* was going to be Air Wing Eleven, assigned to the USS *Abraham Lincoln*. This meant that I would be assigned to squadron VF-213, scheduled to be the next squadron to get the brand-new, smokin' hot, super-powerful F-14D Tomcat, which would feature a new airframe, new and safer engines—the works! *Score!*

Then the Navy cancelled procurement of most of the new F-14Ds. That meant my fleet combat Tomcat squadron, the first that would deploy with women, would now still be flying the older F-14A.

So the Navy switched me from an F-14D training class back to an F-14A training class, which moved my class date up two weeks. To make room in that class, they pulled one of the F-14A students—a guy I had graduated flight school with—and moved him *back* two weeks, to the F-14D class. So he got two weeks off *and* he got to go to the F-14D class. He, not I, would be flying the brand-spankin'-new hot rod.

Think he cared? Not. One. Bit. He thanked me every day for a year.

So, in the skewed world of those who chose to believe it, *that* was my "preferential treatment"—getting moved ahead two weeks. Of course, it wasn't really "preferential" at all. The truth was, I got pulled from my class and sent to fly an older airplane—because I'm a woman.

So that's the story of how, when I declined to return to the controversy and scrutiny of flying the F-14, the Navy put me at the back of the line for an F-18 Hornet assignment to avoid the appearance of preferential treatment. Apparently they forgot I'd already been benched for a year and a half.

I ended up accepting orders in 1996 to be a VIP transport pilot—a plum assignment. But now instead of flying Mach 2, I was transporting admirals and generals all over the country.

A very different flying gig, indeed.

The Near-Death of Hope

The year and a half that I was out of the cockpit almost shattered me. In the time that I rode the bench, I was tossed aside at the fighter wing, waiting for the higher-ups to decide my fate. I was stuck in a manpower office from 0645 to 1700 with what felt like little purposeful work to do other than filing reports and attending meetings. I felt like I was in line for the gallows.

I was no longer flying around with my hair on fire, but I showed up. Meanwhile, gossip was running rampant, and not only across the base; it was newspaper and talk show fodder in San Diego and across the nation. As far as I could see, nobody in the leadership chain was doing anything to publicly discredit the misinformation being spread both locally and nationally. It was devastating, humiliating, and terribly isolating. My squadron wingman were all still on cruise. Although I did have some great Marine Corps friends who were steadfast in their support, I even stopped going to the base gym for a time, because I felt like a pariah and a failure. And yet I had done *nothing wrong*. My emotions fluctuated, ranging from continued hope that the process would move quickly and that sanity would be restored, all the way to despair. I felt as though I was being boiled alive, and I didn't have a say in it.

Certainly, the challenge for the Navy was great, too—especially considering the debacle in the leadership's handling of Kara Hultgreen's crash: Just a month prior to my six-month deployment, I watched *Nightline* as Admiral Robert Spane stated that there was no pilot error involved in her mishap.

No pilot error!

This statement was bold and, I thought, reckless. After all, as cited earlier, 80 to 90 percent of all aviation mishaps contain some element of pilot error. Everyone knew that the scope, the causes, of pilot error were huge; it could be caused by lack of sleep, task overload, a scan breakdown, inadequate nourishment—the list is endless. Admiral Spane could have truthfully said, "Hey, not only is this, hands-down, the toughest airplane in the fleet to land on an aircraft carrier, but it also has compressor-stall issues. When you are only one hundred feet above the water, going 170 miles an hour, if anything goes wrong, your chances of recovery are slim." But instead of revealing this fact, the admiral said there was "no pilot error" involved.

As soon as I heard the admiral's statement, I knew there would be outrage across the fleet; such a blatant disclaimer was highly unusual.

Sure enough, when I got back to the squadron, the level of scrutiny, frustration, and gossip was through the roof. Rarely had a senior ranking officer ever come out and swept aside any chance of pilot error. The admiral's statement didn't sit right with anybody junior to the admiral himself.

Not only that, but it was also a disservice to those of us still flying the F-14 Tomcat. In the previous decade naval aviators had crashed approximately 140 airplanes. We all knew the engines in the F-14A were sketchy at best; they were vulnerable in that power band at that airspeed behind the boat. What every naval aviator, Tomcat pilot, and radar intercept officer really wanted to know was: *If it was not a pilot error—if it was mechanical—can it be fixed? Is it systemic? Will this happen to me? What can we do to prevent it from happening again?*

And above all: *What, for God's sake, are the lessons learned?*

Our lessons learned, our immediate emergency response steps are written in the blood of our friends, our fellow aviators. We all just wanted the truth. But slapping "no pilot error" across the mishap had corrupted the feedback loop and unleashed a shitstorm—especially now that the folks who didn't want women in combat were on the hunt to uncover any perceived impropriety they could find. This just added fuel to that fire.

Meanwhile, I sat in that manpower job, frustrated. I felt stuck. Not knowing what the future held was gut-wrenching. Trapped in silence, I dutifully waited for the chain of command to perform its due diligence in looking at my case. I had no idea it would take as long as it did. I kept hearing not only from my skipper, who had kicked off this whole process, but from others within the Navy's Bureau of Personnel that this was all just a CYA situation because of Kara's mishap and all the bad press.

Maybe so, but it sure was feeling personal. As more time passed, the snowball of bad information kept getting bigger and even more public. It took on a life of its own and turned into a monster. I was twenty-five years old and being vilified in the press for things that weren't true, and I had to sit silently by and watch the whole train wreck happen. I felt scalded, especially when listening to people who didn't even know the facts or what they were talking about. Their self-righteousness and strong, misinformed opinions were driving me crazy. That they tried to use all these incorrect facts to buttress their arguments against women in combat was beyond frustrating. (I later did file a lawsuit, for defamation and invasion of privacy, against the lobbyist. But the courts ruled me a "limited purpose" public figure, meaning that I couldn't legally defend myself against defamation in the way a private citizen could. Why? Not because I was a high-up government official or celebrity—the kind of people who have broad access to media and can defend themselves publicly, the people for whom the "public figure" designation was created. Nope—I was a public figure, the courts said, merely because by being a pioneer in the Navy, I'd put myself in the center of attention. Of course I didn't consider that going into the Navy would require me giving up privacy and the right to defend myself, something none of my male counterparts had to do.)

I realized something during that time, and it became the kernel of my budding awareness, my personal well of resilience: When you are the first one—a pioneer in any endeavor—there is no path to follow. I was making decisions, with little or no experience to draw on, about what to do or not do. I wish someone had been there advising me to speak up and speak out a lot sooner. The American public may not believe everything they hear or see in the press, but it helps to have a balancing opinion; in my case, there was none. Not a single reporter who wrote a negative story about me ever called me or asked to look at my records—not one. I had no way to get my message out or tell my side.

I had stepped up to serve my country. Yet no one bothered to get my side of the story. How accurate could their reporting have been?

The pressure was nearly unbearable. No one in the Navy had ever experienced a public attack this extraordinary, and they didn't know what to do about it . . . so they did nothing. And my span of control felt negligible.

I "flew a desk" at Miramar, waiting for my fate to be decided. I didn't stay in the manpower office the whole time, though (thankfully). I bounced around, from doing a stint on an Admiral's planning staff at "Red Flag" (very challenging), to being a scheduler at the Marine Aviation Weapons and Tactics Squadron in Yuma, Arizona (loved working with the Marines).

But then things got even worse. When the Navy shut down the fighter wing at NAS Miramar, I was transferred over to run the Recycling Division. From routing HR paperwork to routing garbage . . . My career was on an interesting path.

Months after I was benched, one of my squadron mates crashed an airplane for a *second time,* this time with several fatalities involved. The whole squadron stood down. Many aviators didn't fly for weeks as they worked through the stress. This was never an option for me after Kara's mishap. I was expected to get right back in the jet the next day and fly—which I did.

One of my darkest moments occurred during a trip to Washington, DC, to plead my case with a board reviewing my flight status.

If I was to have any chance of getting back my flight status, I had to show up in person. But to add insult to injury, the Navy wouldn't pay for any of my travel or lodging to attend these boards. Washington is a very expensive place to grab a hotel, and I ended up at some fleabag motel in a terrible part of town.

I remember going to a little hole-in-the-wall market nearby to get a "meal": a bottle of Snapple and a Styrofoam container of creamed spinach. I brought it back to my motel room, where the floors were so sticky I didn't dare take off my shoes. As cockroaches skittered to the corners, I plopped in the center of the bed and ate as much of the spinach as I could stomach, thinking, *How in the hell did I end up here?*

I slept with the lights on.

But the next day I got up, put my uniform on, and went to stand proudly before the board. After all, optimism is the greatest form of rebellion.

I could have quit, but I didn't. And a few months later, after standing once again before a flight review board and more admirals who looked more closely at my records, I was finally heading back to the cockpit.

GIVING UP IS THE ONLY WAY TO GUARANTEE YOU WON'T ACHIEVE YOUR DREAM.

Supported by some great wingmen inside BUPERS, back at NAS Miramar and up at MCAS El Toro, I had won my freedom to return to a job I loved. I had even won my reputation—as much as possible after my name had been maligned. Sure, I could have given up. But where would that get me? After all, giving up is the only way to guarantee you won't achieve your dream.

This is why resilience is so important. When faced with a continuously stressful situation, it's easy to lose all hope and just burn out. You become exhausted, mentally and physically. And you come very close to giving up. One of the primary researchers in the field of burnout, psychologist Christina Maslach, has found that high-performance-oriented people who start out very optimistic and idealistic also start their careers with big goals. Upon encountering roadblock after roadblock, however, they *perceive* a lack of personal accomplishment and begin to see themselves as failures.

A sense of achievement and of purpose is important, particularly in your career. Disengagement is soul-sucking. Think of the employees who are stuck in the same position for years because of drawdowns or cutbacks—no promotions, no pay raises, no hope for advancing, self-worth plummeting. The choice is this: Lump it or leave it. Often these people quit—without going anywhere. They never leave the organization, yet they are apathetic, disengaged, a million miles away. Peek under the covers at some major companies, and you'll find plenty of examples of this.

So how do fearless leaders remain resilient when the challenges—whether you're under great pressure, under the microscope, or flying under the radar—seem so great? By leading themselves through adversity.

Seven Steps for Leading Yourself through Adversity

Since I started working with business leaders, I've seen many people squashed by a crucible—but I've also seen many people show great resilience. Those in the latter camp are able to prevent the setback from knocking them off their feet. And in some cases, they turn it around and use it as an advantage.

Dr. Paul Stoltz, chairman of the Global Resilience Institute, surveyed more than one thousand companies in fifty-two countries and found that most of the time (70 to 90 percent), people do a combination of avoiding, surviving, and coping with adversity—meaning that adversity is consuming them. About 10 to 30 percent of the time, people will manage the adversity. Only rarely—5 percent of the time—do people and teams actually harness or leverage adversity and use it to their advantage.[57]

Fearless leaders fall within that 5 percent—and so should you.

The seven steps outlined below have worked for many leaders, including myself, in times of adversity. Use them wisely, and you will find yourself not just surviving your crucible, but thriving.

Step I: Reject Victimhood

We all have to deal with some kind of loss or disappointment in life, whether it's the loss of a dream, the death of a loved one, a serious illness, or the collapse of a venture. In these times, it's tempting to feel that something was stolen from us. It's easy to become discouraged and think, *Ugh, it will always be this way. Things will always be against me.*

You are not alone in these feelings. Assigning blame rather than generating solutions is human nature. But if you get stuck feeling like a victim, you enhance the problem and limit your capacity to get through it.

So, the first step in developing resilience is to reject victimhood. Recognize that we all suffer sometimes, that we all run into roadblocks or just plain get stuck. Those who look at these roadblocks as challenges to be overcome rather than as the slings and arrows of fate are able to stay strong, bounce back, and go on to achieve high performance.

It's so easy to feel sorry for ourselves, especially when we believe we have every right to. But when we internalize our status as a victim, the effect can be devastating. We fall back into limiting beliefs and cocoon ourselves in the comfort zone of the status quo. We become anything but fearless.

When you find yourself facing a crucible, don't let despair and self-pity paralyze you. The situation may feel deeply personal and shockingly unfair, but how you choose to respond to it will determine your success trajectory. Fear doesn't have to hold you back. Get rid of all the *I can'ts, Yeah buts, I should haves,* and *I'll never be able tos.* Determine that you will not be a victim. See your crucible as something that is admittedly terrible and perhaps tragic, but something that is not going to derail you. Whatever it is, remind yourself that it could've happened to anyone. Take a period of downtime to cope, if necessary, but remember to see things in the long term. Do not let this experience turn you into a victim.

Step 2: Embrace Change

Whatever happened to you, happened to you. You can't take it back. You'll be better off if you accept what happened, relegate it to the past, and embrace your new reality, no matter how compromised it seems. That old mantra from AOCS applies here: *Embrace the suck.*

Fearless leaders do this regularly when facing adversity. They realize that no matter what happens, they'll be okay. They may not be happy about it, and they may never regain what they once had, but they will be okay. The resilient among us know that someone out there has it worse, and that getting lost in their own misfortune will do absolutely no good.

So don't drop anchor on the bad stuff. Put your big-boy britches on, accept that the situation happened, and move forward. Your "new normal" might take some getting used to, but you can learn to adapt. As Charles Darwin taught us, survival is guaranteed not for the strongest or most intelligent of a species, but for those of us most responsive to change.

Step 3: Focus on What Matters

When you are a fearless leader, focusing on what matters is paramount to doing a good job; that's why you have to create a vision for your team to align with. But when you or your team faces a crucible, laser-like focus becomes more important than ever. You've got this giant weight on your shoulders, but you have to find a way to still keep your eye on the ball. People are still relying on you.

So start with the big picture. Take a quick inventory. What do you see from the thirty-thousand-foot level? Sometimes you have to go even higher, maybe to eighty thousand feet. First, are you alive? Okay, then you're still in the game. I am not being sarcastic here. When your world is crumbling around you—because of a death in a family, the loss of a limb, divorce—tomorrow doesn't even seem tolerable, let alone getting through today. But if you're alive, there's reason to hope.

Then, when you feel as though you can breathe again—and maybe make it until lunchtime—step it down a little. Zoom in on what *really* matters to you: your core values, your purpose. What are the most important parts of your life today? Family? Work? Community? Self-development? The legacy you want to leave? Things might not look so great right now, but if you have embraced your new reality and can focus now on what matters most to you, you're on your way to making a comeback.

Now analyze your part or role in the new reality, and plan your course of action. What are the next steps? Focus your time and attention on those few things. When you have too many priorities, it's easy to become overwhelmed, overloaded, and hopeless. Focus on what matters! As we say in fighter aviation, "If you lose sight, you lose the fight."

Step 4: Find a Wingman

Emotional support during times of crisis is critical, and communication is key. Once you've stabilized your free fall, surround yourself with great wingmen, and stay engaged. High achievers and peak performers can be wickedly independent and driven. After all, that is why they are so successful! But everyone—even the badasses—needs support.

Spend time with people who will listen while you talk and who will provide positive support. For some people (myself included) seeking out support, *asking for help*, can be very hard to do. It makes you feel vulnerable, and *vulnerable* feels like a four-letter word—but it's not. Asking for help is an admirable choice—and one of the hardest things for high achievers to do. Don't be afraid to pick up the phone or sit down and actually *talk* to somebody. So often our default these days is to use email or texts, but be warned—they are a poor substitute for personal interaction.

Step 5: Know What You Can Control

The next step to becoming more resilient is understanding your span of control. Don't waste your time and energy trying to change circumstances you can't control. Accepting the things you cannot change allows you to focus on the things you *do* have control over. Even if you can't change a stressful situation, you have a choice in how you respond. Ask, "What *can* be done?"

I'm going to share with you an example that hits close to home for me—and has heavily influenced my views on resilience.

Though he probably doesn't know it, my cousin Charlie Lemon is my hero. At twenty-six years old, Charlie enlisted in the US Army, in combat arms. As an Abrams tank soldier, he deployed in 2010 to Iraq. About ten months into deployment, while out on a routine mission, his truck was hit by an improvised explosive device—an IED. Charlie was standing in the truck. The penetrator went through his legs and also killed his best friend.

Although the truck wasn't badly damaged, the devastation to Charlie physically was profound. He fought for his life over the course of the next few weeks and endured many surgeries in the months that followed. He ended up losing both of his legs.

Yet Charlie has managed with grace the new deck of cards he was dealt. In fact, he has grabbed life by the horns. He now cycles and races all over the world with Operation Comfort. He has done 500-mile races, and he keeps pushing through barriers. He surfs, he fishes, he stays engaged. His next goal is to make the US Paralympics team.

Instead of doubting his capabilities and getting mired in longing for what used to be, Charlie strives to answer the question *What can be done?* To do anything less would have been self-limiting. By taking charge of what he can control, he has been able to bounce back and go beyond the typical expectations, exhibiting astounding resilience not just mentally but physically. He has chosen to push ahead and define life on his terms, while blasting through barriers. Some of the most poignant words about his resilience come from

Charlie's mom: "Some people never even get to meet a hero. I am proud to say that I got to raise one. I have been truly blessed to be a military mom." Amen.

Rather than dwelling on a factor he can't control, Charlie decided he wanted to live a life that is, as he says, "worthy of my best friend's sacrifice." Mission accomplished, Charlie.

Step 6: Learn from Adversity

To achieve continued high performance or success, you must get out of your comfort zone and choose to do new things, and that means you *will* fail. That's right—failure is not an *if,* but a *when.* You know what the threat of failure feels like: anxiety, discomfort, fear. You want to hide, or maybe let someone else go first and see how it all works out for him! That's the safe path . . . and it's bullshit. It will keep you playing small, scared, and resentful. It will allow you to wallow in the past rather than move into the future.

> **TO ACHIEVE CONTINUED HIGH PERFORMANCE OR SUCCESS, YOU MUST GET OUT OF YOUR COMFORT ZONE AND CHOOSE TO DO NEW THINGS, AND THAT MEANS YOU *WILL* FAIL.**

As a fearless leader, when you get thrown off course, instead of seeing yourself as a failure, you have to view it as a learning opportunity. You have to learn from what you've just been through, figure out what went wrong—*even if you didn't have control of the situation*—and then integrate the life lesson. Having a coping strategy like this will up your resilience factor. One of the strengths of most fighter pilots is that we are able to do one thing exceptionally well: understand our mistakes and then fix them. We constantly strive to take corrective action.

Just as the Prepare-Perform-Prevail process ends with a debrief, so should your struggle with adversity. You can use the power of questions to gain focus and learn valuable lessons. Look for the root cause of a problem, and then brainstorm solutions. Ask, "What happened? How can I turn this around? Why is it good that this happened?" Discern the value in the experience. Maybe, if possible, you can even find a little humor in the situation.

Step 7: Take Action!

Finally, look forward and take action! Take those lessons learned, and—despite feeling afraid, anxious, disappointed, or completely screwed over—move quickly from analysis to your plan of action. Respond. Be intentional. Feel the fear, and do it anyway. Nobody can prevent you from choosing to move forward and be exceptional.

Do something specific that can lead to a more positive outcome. It may start with picking up the phone or just getting out of bed, but whatever it is, keep moving forward. When in doubt, go get your mantra tattooed on your wrist. No, really! You'll see it every day, and it'll be a reminder that you are still here—you are still *in the game*. But you have to choose to be.

When you get hit with adversity, it's important to take stock and then keep moving. Find the opportunities hidden within the obstacles. Do something positive with what happened to you. Those who survive and thrive are able to turn setbacks into successes and roadblocks into stepping-stones. Fearless leaders discover meaning in every mishap, and they emerge not just stronger but better equipped with tools to lead and to learn.

FEEL THE FEAR. AND DO IT ANYWAY.

Sure, it would be nice if you could simply snap your fingers and automatically become more resilient, but it doesn't happen overnight. However, if you take positive, decisive action, you can improve your capacity to withstand adversity, bounce back from setbacks, and not only survive, but thrive!

Remember: Feel the fear. And do it anyway.

Post-traumatic Growth

Understanding resilience is critical—and it can help you recover more quickly from a traumatic experience of any kind.

You've heard of post-traumatic stress disorder—PTSD. It affects almost 8 million American adults.[58] It can occur at almost any age, including in children. PTSD sufferers may be victims of physical, emotional, or sexual assault; accidents; natural disasters; military combat; or overwhelming, continuous stress that causes hopelessness. Not everyone who has PTSD has physically been through the event; some people experience symptoms when a loved one goes through a traumatic occurrence. Then there are the secondary stressors that add to the original trauma, sometimes causing depression, anxiety, withdrawal from normal activity, insomnia, and substance abuse.

As a steady stream of veterans return from the Iraq and Afghanistan wars, there has been a lot of discussion and attention surrounding PTSD, and that's a good thing. The more people are aware of the symptoms, the sooner they can recognize and understand what is happening to them and those closest to them—and the sooner they can get help if needed.

But we are missing out on a huge part of the conversation.

Have you heard of post-traumatic growth? Yes, PTG. It's a real term, a real condition, but my guess is that you're unfamiliar with it. In the past year, I've asked thousands of people in my audiences whether they've heard of PTG. Only one hand has gone up. Clearly we are missing out on one of the key elements of bouncing back.

Research shows that only a very small percentage of people actually suffer long-term effects of PTSD after a traumatic event. (To be clear, PTSD is different from traumatic brain injury, which poses its own set of challenges.) The majority of us, given the right support, are able to put the event into a better context and actually come through it stronger—with an improved sense of self, better relationships, recognition of new opportunities, and a greater appreciation for life. Recovery from adversity, and bouncing back to become even stronger, takes a bit of time, but it can—and should—happen for the majority of people.

Adversity, when met with the right attitude, can be a catalyst for growth. Difficulties and misfortune oftentimes define your strengths and weaknesses for you, whether you like it or not. You just have to be able to apply the lessons learned. The awareness gained from overcoming adversity plays a crucial role in your path to success. What you think of now as a big disappointment or huge stumbling block can actually be the launching pad to something greater.

Most people underestimate their ability to recover from trauma. As we have more in-depth conversations around PTSD, we must point out the potential for PTG. Remaining resilient is critical to reengaging with life. The long-term effects of resilience on performance and mental health are staggering—as are the effects when a person is unable to bounce back. For fearless leaders, understanding what it takes to develop those resilience skills and mindset among your teammates is critical.

As Elie Wiesel said, "There are victories of the soul and spirit. Sometimes, even if you lose, you win." With some effort, you can find the silver lining, the positive way forward, in any adversity. You can take a lot more than you think you can. You can do things you never dreamed possible!

Life after Mach 2

Clearly, life goes on. It was with no small irony that I wrapped up my Navy career right where it started: at Naval Air Station Pensacola. It was here that the hopes and dreams of many have been tested, where those dreams were crushed or lifted as we ran, studied, struggled, pushed past our limits, and learned to be fantastic teammates, wing-men, and naval officers. Near the end of my military career, I ran the same woodchip trail to the lighthouse that I had run as an officer candidate. It was the same place where I learned how to adapt in any situation . . . how to overcome any obstacle thrown my way . . . how to handle challenges with grace and not lose my military bearing. And perhaps most of all, how to bounce back and come away stronger, more aware, and more empathetic. How to be more resilient.

The battalion building, where we slept, studied, and did countless mountain climbers, still sparkled. Someone continued to polish the brass on the cannons outside the front door. I even dared to go in to see if the DI's office was still there—it was. I could hear the bellowing voice of Gunnery Sergeant Woodring in my head as though it were yesterday. I watched the magical Navy Blue Angels practice regularly over the field, this time with a cup of coffee in my hand instead of only being able to sneak a peek out of the corner of my eye as an aviation officer candidate, hoping one day I would be fortunate enough to fly a high-performing aircraft like that. It was one of the bonuses of having my office right in Base Ops; I had the best seat in the whole house.

Life was good—different, but good. The sting of what had happened during my year-and-a-half on the bench was not gone—but I was flying again.

I embraced the change. I loved being able to fly the Navy's top brass around, and Marine Corps and Air Force top generals, too. We were always going to different places, different airfields. The flying was good, and the folks that I worked with were awesome. As always, it was great to be airborne, and to be surrounded and supported by awesome wingmen.

Unfortunately this time, too, ended much too soon, thanks to more fiscal cutbacks—not something I could control. Our base was losing our airplanes, and all the pilots needed to get another flying job somewhere else. The other pilots in my squadron had no problem, but once again I ran into roadblocks. When I requested to be transferred up to NAS Memphis, I was quickly told by a Navy captain at the Bureau of Personnel that there was no airplane at that base for me to fly. He didn't say there were no orders available; he said there was *no airplane*. Interestingly enough, two of the guys from my squadron had just received orders to fly there.

For months the discussion went back and forth. My squadron commander was strongly advocating for me. Even the captain of NAS Pensacola—the base skipper, a former F-14 RIO—got involved, trying to make something happen for me. But the Bureau of Personnel wasn't budging. They said my only option was a three-year set of orders to Japan. I was beyond disappointed; moving my family thousands of miles away was out of the question—my husband was flying for FedEx and based in Memphis, which meant I would be heading to Japan as a single mother. Not optimal. By this time the guys I had been flying with at NAS Pensacola were already flying up in Memphis . . . you know, the place that didn't have an airplane.

The writing on the wall was clear to me: My time in the Navy was coming to an end. I took a set of one-year non-flying orders and finished my time in the Navy working for the admiral at the Naval Education and Training Center, where I learned a lot about training in the Navy and about developing training programs. But my heart was in the cockpit—and that heart was a little broken.

It's said that everything happens for a reason, even if we don't understand the reason at the time, even when we feel broken, betrayed, defeated. In my time on the bench, I had my first daughter, and of course she was (and is) amazing—a gift. On more than one occasion during my darkest days, I was able to look at her and think, *You are the reason why I can say, "I wouldn't go back and change anything."* Otherwise, I would've never had *her*—a child at some point, perhaps, but not her. The same goes for the rest of my children.

WHEN YOU COME FACE-TO-FACE WITH HARDSHIP OR SUFFER A SEVERE SETBACK, YOU GET TO CHOOSE HOW YOU WILL RESPOND.

When you come face-to-face with hardship or suffer a severe setback, you get to choose how you will respond. Choose well, and you may just find yourself with some of the most formidable opportunities life has to offer. Whether it's a personal or a professional setback, life will go on. Embrace the change, thorns and all. Find a great wingman, understand what you can influence, grab those lessons learned, and move on stronger and better for having had the experience.

Leading Your Team through Adversity

Now you know how, thanks to my very own adversity training—my crucible—I've learned to be even more resilient. Earlier in this chapter, we looked at how *you* can become resilient too—and building a resilient *team* should be part of your focus. So let's explore how the topics covered in previous chapters will make for a more resilient team.

In this turbulent business environment, leadership requires taking bold steps. No matter what challenges your organization is facing—a slowing economy, a merger, new rules and regulations—the pace of change has never been faster. The sheer unpredictability of things can cause fear and anxiety among your team. Your job as a fearless leader is to throttle back the stress your team is feeling, to help them to be more agile, and to ensure that they are able to survive and win.

Here are some ways you can boost your team's resilience and help them shine in tough circumstances.

Clarify the Win

When the winds of change blow in, in order to stay on track as you are getting buffeted about, continue opening the lines of communication. Ask your team, "What are we striving for?" When people are engaged with clear and meaningful goals, they have greater resilience and are more likely to see a challenge as an opportunity. Remind them what the win looks like, and warn them that there will be peaks and valleys. Your whole team may be cruising along, happy as clams—and suddenly get kicked in the teeth by the unexpected. I've been there, and it's not pretty. Grab a box of Kleenex, wipe your eyes and nose, and ask one another, "Okay, what next?" Remember why you started—and remind your team often.

Know Your Team

Your people are your biggest asset. Remember those "kids" who operate on that flight deck twenty-four hours a day, seven days a week, helping keep us pilots alive? You may be surprised to learn how much the average Air Boss knows about his shipmates who are working the deck. In between flight operations, you can often find the Air Boss chatting with the troops. I know this from watching flight ops up in the tower, hearing the bosses make funny comments over the flight deck radio for all to hear. Getting to know the kids on the deck is smart leadership. When the time comes to push that crew through crappy visibility, unbearable heat, or long stretches of uninterrupted flight operations, those teammates will feel valued—they will feel *human*.

YOU CAN'T EXPECT YOUR TEAM TO BLINDLY FOLLOW YOUR LEADERSHIP IF YOU HAVEN'T BOTHERED TO INVEST ANY TIME GETTING TO KNOW THEM.

You can't expect your team to blindly follow your leadership if you haven't bothered to invest any time getting to know them. A real human connection builds a solid foundation for the times when you really need your team to power through an extreme situation.

Before a presentation with clients, I always spend time getting to know them, weeks before the event. What matters to them? What obstacles are they facing? What are they trying to achieve? But when discussing these ideas with executive teams, sometimes I'll hear, "That's just not possible—I'm too busy to do that." Yet you're not too busy to ask your people for extended working hours, or pay cuts, or to "manage change," or to make other sacrifices. If you want a resilient team, you need to *build* one. The least you can do is make an effort to understand what drives your teammates.

Fearless leadership is a people business. It's about getting your team together to do the impossible while keeping their health, sanity, and even humor intact. Fearless leaders always put the team first, and these team members know they are valued. Valued teammates will go to the mat for you, and you probably won't even have to ask.

A business team in the pursuit of excellence may not face the same physical dangers and challenges as a fighter pilot or a Navy SEAL, but aspirational goals—the big bets—will require the same courage, tenacity, integrity, perseverance, and flexibility. Overcoming obstacles like chronic stress requires resilience. Choosing people with the right skills, talent, training, and *attitude* is essential. Without mutual support and trust, your team will get nowhere.

Prepare Relentlessly

Now that you know your goal and your team, the question to ask is: How do you achieve results consistently, even if you face adversity? The answer is simple: through relentless preparation and training. Insistence on preparation is one of the priceless gifts a fearless leader can offer his or her team. Being prepared alleviates pressure because your teammates not only know what to expect—they have already prepared how they will respond to any challenge the environment (or the competition) throws their way. This promotes resilience by increasing their ability to adapt and overcome barriers.

Continue that cycle of Prepare-Perform-Prevail, even on the fly. Adjust and adapt, adjust and adapt, adjust and adapt—over and over, even while navigating the choppy waters of a crisis. Help your team stay focused on both near-term priorities and long-term goals. It's like that circus trick of having one foot on two different galloping horses. Successful teams are able to do this because they have done whatever is necessary to prepare.

Remember the Navy saying: *Train like you fight.* Increase your team's coping skills and resilience by practicing over and over. You can't think that when stress pays a visit, your team will just magically rise to the occasion; you have to prepare them to do so. Grittiness is earned.

Continue Learning

When change happens, uncertainty and ambiguity can paralyze your team. Fear sets in, caution envelops us, and instead of strapping into our fighter jet and going for it, we curl up and wait for the storm to pass, for things to settle down. But what if this change in your environment is your team's new normal? You don't have the luxury of waiting for things to blow over. To remain relevant, you must learn quickly by continuing the open dialogue about what is working and what isn't. Find a way forward—or make one. Create your own future by *taking action.* Don't be a passenger in your own life, and don't let your team's future flail in the wind. Take risks and learn from your mistakes.

Culture Matters

The culture you promote as a leader could be one of the biggest barriers to success, even more so than the talents (or the lack thereof) of your teammates. When the chips are down, if you punish people who innovate or who dare to go first—or if you don't reward those who build and maintain a strong team—you won't attract and retain the types of people who can make stuff happen in a volatile environment.

Period. You will quickly lose any competitive advantage, and your current success level will most likely start to slip.

You can't talk about innovation without understanding that risk is inherent. When you're trying something new, it will get messy; rarely is something new done perfectly the first time. Nor can you give lip service to leadership development or "growing your people" or encouraging your team to be "on the leading edge" if you're simply going to shove them off a cliff at the first sign of a struggle. Instead, as a fearless leader, you must understand that culture matters—that *you* are the one responsible for growing and developing more resilient people and fostering a more resilient team.

Fearless leaders understand the importance of building a resilient, high-performing team. Resilience on an individual level can fluctuate from time to time depending on external events in the lives of your employees or teammates. But by promoting the right culture—with your team aligned on a common objective and maintaining a high level of mutual trust and optimism—you can ensure unwavering resilience on a team level. Resilient teams are able to weather the chronic, high stress of a constantly changing and challenging environment—and those teams will always be more productive and successful in the long run.

*   *   *

On your journey to becoming the best you and the best leader you can be, the single most powerful piece of advice I can give to you is: *Be fearless.* Follow whatever dream you have, and believe that it is enough. You will run into roadblocks, challenges, and naysayers. But you and you alone have the power to choose whether adversity will destroy you or make you better. Only *you* can decide to be resilient.

There are people who sit in the bleachers, who criticize, condemn, and judge. These folks have never stepped into the ring, and I'm done giving them much more thought. There will always be trolls. There will always be those who comment anonymously, who are too afraid to go for it themselves but are quite willing to tear you down for even daring to try.

People constantly ask, "Was it worth it?" My answer: Absolutely. I love naval aviation, and I believe in the Navy's core values of Honor, Courage, and Commitment. I believe in the people who dedicate their lives to something greater than themselves, who work to push themselves to the limits, who are willing to live with a devotion to courage, to fearlessness. To the men and women I served with who chose to do so with dignity, integrity, and grace: I salute you. To the country that allowed me the opportunity to serve: I am forever grateful.

The best of life's lessons don't have to be learned in the cockpit, going Mach 2 with your hair on fire. But I wouldn't choose to have it any other way.

Conclusion

BE FEARLESS!

I hope you have enjoyed the high-performance lessons learned shared in this book.

More crucially, I hope you have benefitted from them, and that you now understand that you do not need permission to be fearless, to go after what you want.

Most people give up too soon when pursuing their goals, growing their teams or chasing their dreams. Fearless leadership doesn't develop in an instant; it develops over the course of time.

The lessons that I learned and shared with you will only make a difference—a lasting positive impact, if you go out and take bold action.

For the next thirty days, think about what is possible and then start *taking action* to make your dreams, your future a reality. You must *do* something different for this to happen. Sitting around hoping, wishing, dreaming of a better future for yourself or your team will not magically make stuff happen. Be intentional, be tenacious, be resilient and be courageous. Bold, fearless action drives success.

Your challenge is to confront your fears, to summon up the courage in spite of your fears and go for it anyway. Get comfortable being uncomfortable. You learn to be fearless by living—not by being afraid.

Fearless leadership is the difference between creating the life, or the organization that you want, and settling.

We are only here for a little while. No matter where you are in the leadership journey, risk more, worry less and don't settle.

Be fearless.

ACKNOWLEDGMENTS

I offer my deepest gratitude to the countless people who helped make this book a reality.

I am grateful and privileged to have worked and served with so many wonderfully talented people, both in the US Navy and in my time since. I've had the pleasure of working with people from all different organizations and walks of life who challenged me to step into myself, and to look even more deeply at what matters.

Although I can never thank everyone, I can thank a few.

Christa Haberstock of See Agency. I am blessed to have a world-class agent who also happens to be a fantastic friend. For your unvarnished advice and guidance, and enthusiastic support, thank you. God bless ya, Christa.

Clint Greenleaf, for your encouragement, patience, and faith in not only this book, but in me as well. The Greenleaf Book Group team is simply magnificent.

Aaron Hierholzer, my editor who helped push me to be a better writer, and who kept me sane in the writing process under tight deadlines and some extraordinary circumstances. Your commitment and meticulous attention to detail rivals that of any fighter pilot. You need a call sign . . .

Joe Calloway, for your mentorship, friendship, and precious advice in helping me uncover my voice. "Just be you . . ."

Allison Rodgers, my phenomenally talented photographer. Your crazy skills are only eclipsed by how darn *nice* you are. Nice is good. It's the new black . . .

My loyal friends, thank you for your patience and for always giving me a BS-free perspective while remaining supportive. I am blessed. I thank all of you; now it's time to ring the bell!

No thank-you would seem adequate for my family. My parents. Every day I miss my Dad. But I am grateful for my parents instilling in me the values of hard work, pursuing excellence, and the importance of treating everyone with respect, no matter rank, position or title. For embracing my persistence and desire to always be pushing the limits. I'm sure at times it wasn't easy. But you gave me the greatest gift ever: you believed in me.

My brother Steve for "tolerating" me constantly tagging along—from pee-wee hockey to the University of Wisconsin (Sunday dinners were the best) and all the way through flight school. Thanks for being so awesome.

Donovan Lohrenz, my husband. I could not have finished this book without your love and support. From stepping in to run our four kids around during marathon writing sessions, to listening to me voice my own vulnerabilities, fears, and doubts during this endeavor. You deserve a medal. Or a vacation. I'll let you choose.

My kids. Thank you for being a constant source of love and inspiration to practice what I preach. The book is done. Someday you can read it. Not today. Today we play. And we play big!

And to you the reader, I thank you for trusting me with your time. There will always be barriers to our success and obstacles to overcome. Persevere.

A portion of the proceeds from this book will be donated to veteran nonprofit organizations.

ENDNOTES

Chapter 1

1 Dharmesh Shah, "9 Qualities of Truly Confident People," blog at Linke-
dIn.com, June 6, 2013, https://www.linkedin.com/today/post/
article/20130606150641-658789-9-qualities-of-truly-confident-people.

2 Richard D. Arvey, Maria Rotundo, Wendy Johnson, Zhen Zhang, and Matt McGue, "The
Determinants of Leadership Role Occupancy: Genetic and Personality Factors," *The Leadership
Quarterly* 17 (2006).

3 "Leading with Confidence," presentation from Connect: Professional Women's Network,
http://www.slideshare.net/Women_Connect/leading-with-confidence.

4 Ruth Malloy, "Don't Let Your Career 'Just Happen,'" September 6, 2013, *Harvard Business
Review* Blog Network, http://blogs.hbr.org/2013/09/dont-let-your-career-just-happ/.

5 James R. Mahalik, Elisabeth B. Morray, Aimee Coonerty-Femiano, Larry H. Ludlow, Suzanne
M. Slattery, and Andrew Smiler, "Development of the Conformity to Feminine Norms Inventory," *Sex Roles* 52, no. 7/8 (April 2005).

6 Carol Dweck, *Mindset: The New Psychology of Success* (New York: Random House, 2006), p. 7.

7 Drew Houston, commencement speech at Massachusetts Institute of Technology, June 7, 2013, transcript accessed at http://bostinno.streetwise.co/2013/06/07/
transcript-of-drew-houstons-speech-at-2013-mit-graduation/.

8   Jennifer Robison, "Experiences That Help Emerging Leaders Grow," February 8, 2013, *Gallup Business Journal*, http://businessjournal.gallup.com/content/160295/experiences-help-emerging-leaders-grow.aspx.

9   Susan Jeffers, "The Five Truths About Fear," http://www.susanjeffers.com/home/5truths.cfm.

Chapter 2

10   Gary Vaynerchuk, "Get Your F**king Shovel!" author's Medium blog, September 3, 2013, https://medium.com/this-happened-to-me/dd4a3f7901d0.

11   Karl E. Weick, *Sensemaking in Organizations* (Thousand Oaks, CA: Sage Publications, 1995), 54.

12   Jeff Wise, "What's the Scariest Part of a Frightening Experience?" Extreme Fear (blog) on PyschologyToday.com, March 11, 2010, http://www.psychologytoday.com/blog/extreme-fear/201003/whats-the-scariest-part-frightening-experience.

Chapter 3

13   James B. Stockdale, *Thoughts of a Philosophical Fighter Pilot* (Stanford, CA: Hoover Institution Press, 1995), 69.

14   Stockdale, *Thoughts of a Philosophical Fighter Pilot*, 69.

15   US Army War College, "Study on Military Professionalism," June 30, 1970, http://www.carlisle.army.mil/USAWC/dclm/pdf/study1970.pdf.

16   C. Anne Bonen, *"Professionalism" from Lieutenants to Colonels—A 1981 Attitudinal Assessment among SOS, ACSC, and AWC Students* (Maxwell AFB, Alabama: Air Command and Staff College, 1981), ix.

17   Joseph R. Daskevich and Paul A. Nafziger, T*he Pulse of Professionalism, ACSC AY* 80 (Maxwell AFB, Alabama: Air Command and Staff College, 1980), vii.

18   American Management Association, *AMA 2002 Corporate Values Survey* (New York: AMA, 2002).

19   Joanne B. Ciulla, *Ethics: The Heart of Leadership* (Westport, CT: Praeger Publishers, 1998), 28.

20   M. McCall and M. Lombardo, *Off the Track: Why and How Successful Executives Get Derailed*, Technical Report 21 (Greensboro, NC: Center for Creative Leadership, 1983).

21   AP-GfK poll, November 2013, http://ap-gfkpoll.com/main/wp-content/uploads/2013/11/AP-GfK-October-2013-Poll-Topline-Final_TRUST.pdf.

22   Connie Cass, "In God We Trust, Maybe, But Not Each Other," ap-gfkpoll.com, November 30, 2013, http://ap-gfkpoll.com/featured/our-latest-poll-findings-24.

23   Ibid.

24   Glen Llopis, "7 Reasons Employees Don't Trust Their Leaders," *Forbes*, December 9, 2013, http://www.forbes.com/sites/glennllopis/2013/12/09/7-reasons-employees-dont-trust-their-leaders/.

25   Adam Bryant, "Dolf van den Brink of Heineken USA, on Transparency," *New York Times*, November 26, 2013.

26   Daniel Roberts, "Dolf van den Brink Stands Fast with Heineken," CNN Money, September 25, 2013, http://money.cnn.com/2013/09/19/magazines/fortune/40-under-40-van-den-brink.pr.fortune/.

27   Adam Bryant, "Jennifer Dulski of Change.org, on Problem-Solving," *New York Times*, November 30, 2013.

28   Joanna Lamphere Beckham, "Not Self, But Country," *Vanderbilt Magazine*, Fall 2010.

29   Karel Montor, ed., *Naval Leadership: Voices of Experience* (Annapolis, MD: Naval Institute Press, 1998), 71.

30   HBR Blog Network, "The Biggest Mistake a Leader Can Make," video, August 31, 2010, http://blogs.hbr.org/2010/08/the-biggest-mistake-a-leader-c/.

31   Richard Finger, "Why American Airlines Employees Loathe Management," *Forbes*, April 29, 2013.

32   Anthony Castellano, "Judge Allows Hostess to Give Executives $1.8M in Bonuses," ABC News, November 30, 2012, http://abcnews.go.com/Business/judge-hostess-give-executives-18m-bonuses/story?id=17844113.

33   Kyle Stock, "Barclays, Still Paying Handsomely, Cutting 12,000 Positions," *Businessweek*, February 11, 2014, http://www.businessweek.com/articles/2014-02-11/barclays-still-paying-handsomely-cutting-12-000-positions.

34   Dan Carrison and Rod Walsh, *Semper Fi: Business Leadership the Marine Corps Way* (New York: AMACOM, 2005).

35   Zac Bissonnette, *Good Advice from Bad People* (New York: Penguin, 2014).

36   William A. Cohen, *A Class with Drucker* (New York: AMACOM, 2008), 90.

37   William A. Cohen, "Absolute Integrity Is the Basis of Heroic Leadership," *Leader to Leader* 59 (Winter 2011): 46–47.

38   Perry M. Smith and Jeffrey W. Foley, *Rules & Tools for Leaders* (New York: Perigee, 2013), 22.

Chapter 4

39 Katrina Schwartz, "Age of Distraction: Why It's Crucial for Students to Learn to Focus," KQED's MindShift (blog), December 5, 2013, http://blogs.kqed.org/mindshift/2013/12/age-of-distraction-why-its-crucial-for-students-to-learn-to-focus/.

40 Walter Isaacson, "The Real Leadership Lessons of Steve Jobs," *Harvard Business Review*, April 2012, http://hbr.org/2012/04/the-real-leadership-lessons-of-steve-jobs/ar/1.

41 Karl E. Weick, *Sensemaking in Organizations* (Thousand Oaks, CA: Sage Publications, 1995), 55.

42 Deloitte, *Culture of Purpose: A Business Imperative*, 2013 Core Beliefs and Culture Survey, http://www.deloitte.com/assets/Dcom-UnitedStates/Local%20Assets/Documents/us_leadership_2013corebeliefs&culturesurvey_051613.pdf.

43 Bill McCarthy, in discussion with the author.

44 Jack Dorsey, interviewed by Lara Logan, *60 Minutes*, CBS, March 2013.

Chapter 5

45 Adam Bryant, "Phil Martens of Novelis, on Consistent Leadership," *New York Times*, October 26, 2013.

46 J. Keith Murnighan, "Micro Managers: Learn to Trust Your People," CNN.com, August 25, 2012, http://www.cnn.com/2012/08/24/opinion/micro-manager-trust-murnighan/.

47 Gert-Jan Pepping, Geir Jordat, and Tjerk Moll, "Emotional Contegion in Soccer Penalty Shortcuts: Celebration of Individual Success Is Associated with Ultimate Team Success, *Journal of Sports Sciences* 28(9): 983–92.

48 Kathleen O'Toole, "Behavior Lessons for Leadership and Teamwork," Stanford Graduate School of Business website, March 20, 2012, http://www.gsb.stanford.edu/news/headlines/gruenfeld-power-2012.html.

49 W. James McNerney Jr., "How We're Going to Improve Performance: Highlights from 2005 Earnings Conference Call with Analysts and Media," February 1, 2006, http://www.boeing.com/news/speeches/2006/mcnerney_060201.html.

50 Kim Peterson, "Why Amazon Pays Employees $5,000 to Quit," CBS MoneyWatch, April 11, 2014, http://www.cbsnews.com/news/amazon-pays-employees-5000-to-quit/.

51 Garry Kranz, "More Firms Paying Mind to Mentoring," *Workforce Management* 89, no. 1, January 2010.

52 Michael Donovan, "Executives: Why Even Consider a Mentoring Program for Your Business," Evan Carmichael.com, http://www.evancarmichael.com/Business-Coach/197/Why-even-consider-a-Mentoring-Program-for-Your-Business.html.

Chapter 6

53   Carmine Gallo, "Employee Motivation the Ritz-Carlton Way," *Businessweek*, February 29, 2008, http://www.businessweek.com/stories/2008-02-29/employee-motivation-the-ritz-carl-ton-waybusinessweek-business-news-stock-market-and-financial-advice.

54   Scott Shappell, Cristy Detwiler, Kali Holcomb, Carla Hackworth, Cristina Bates, Albert Boquet, Douglas Wiegmann, *Human Error and Commercial Aviation Accidents: A Comprehensive, Fine-Grained Analysis Using HFACS*, Report Number DOT/FAA/AM-05/24 (Washington, DC: Office of Aerospace Medicine, 2006), http://www.hf.faa.gov/docs/508/docs/gaFY05HFACS.pdf.

Chapter 7

55   "Department of Defense Human Factors Analysis and Classification System," http://www.uscg.mil/safety/docs/mab_nonaviation/dod_hfacs_list_and_definition.doc.

56   George A. Miller, "The Magical Number Seven, Plus or Minus Two," *The Psychological Review* 63, 1956, 81_97.

57   Paul Stoltz, "When Adversity Strikes, What Do You Do?" *Harvard Business Review*, July 7, 2010, http://blogs.hbr.org/2010/07/when-adversity-strikes-what-do/.

58   "PTSD: A Growing Epidemic," *NIH MedlinePlus* 4, no. 1 (Winter 2009): 10–14.